DRAWING and PERCEIVING

DRAWING *and* PERCEIVING

Life Drawing for Students of Architecture and Design

THIRD EDITION

Douglas Cooper

JOHN WILEY & SONS, INC.

New York • Chichester • Weinheim • Brisbane • Singapore • Toronto

When they first begin taking classes with me, a large portion of my students have never taken a prior drawing course. Their feelings must be something close to what I might feel if I were to suddenly—heaven forbid—take up ballet. I dedicate this book to these students. It is from them, the ones who have started with the least, that I have experienced my greatest joys as a teacher.

Coca-Cola®, Coke®, the Dynamic Ribbon device, and the contour bottle are all trademarks of the Coca-Cola Company.

Library of Congress Cataloging-in-Publication Data:

Cooper, Douglas, 1946–
    Drawing and perceiving : life drawing for students of architecture and design /
  Douglas Cooper. — 3rd ed.
      p.   cm.
    Includes index.
    ISBN 0-471-35714-6 (pbk. : alk. paper)
    1. Architectural drawing—Technique. 2. Visual perception. I. Title.

NA2708.C66 2000
720'.28'4—dc21   99-089639

Printed in the United States of America.

10 9 8 7 6 5 4 3 2

Contents

Preface

For instructor resources,
point your web browser to:
**http://www.wiley.com/products/
subject/architecture/archdesign/
cooper/index.html**

Recently I heard a story from an alumnus of Carnegie Mellon University about the great Beaux Arts architect and designer of the original Carnegie Tech campus, Henry Hornbostel. Hornbostel had also served as the first Dean of Carnegie Tech's College of Fine Arts.

It seems he had been brought into a design competition for a major public commission at the end of the process because the jury was dissatisfied by the entrants' submissions. The jurors were hoping they might get some inspiring ideas from Hornbostel, and so they invited him to inspect the site from an overlooking hill. Hornbostel had huge hands. And so when they asked him what he might propose, he simply whipped out his left hand, took a pen in his right, and there on his tablet-sized hand proceeded to draw a perspective rendering of what he might do. The amazed jury nearly awarded him the commission right there on the spot.

It has been almost ten years since I wrote the second edition of *Drawing and Perceiving,* and I have come to believe that what is most important for students in design fields is exactly the sort of drawing that Hornbostel demonstrated on that hill long ago: drawing that is second nature; drawing that is quick; drawing that can win the commission; drawing that

comes right out of the finger tips, straight from a knowledge of the real physical world. And that sort of freehand drawing is all the more important in the computer age, now that most of the work of perspective construction is no longer necessary. So the question is: how to get this ability?

It doesn't happen overnight. Courses that emphasize expression at the expense of observation miss the point. And it doesn't come from drawing that emphasizes appearance over three-dimensional understanding. Hornbostel could draw convincingly from that hilltop because he understood the three-dimensional implications of the marks he set down. His was not a painterly understanding. It was informed by years of building and years of drawing what he built.

I believe drawing ability comes from three sources. It arises in the hand—almost as an athletic issue, the hand must move well. It arises in the intellect—the structure of the world must be understood. And it arises in conception—ultimately, drawing must impart order to what is drawn. I have tried in this third edition to address these three aspects: the first chapter addressing the body, the second the mind, and the third the spirit.

Acknowledgments

Teaching begins and ends with students. Their successes are the great pleasure of teaching. Over the years, I have taught more than 2,000 students, and their drawings are the heart of this work. I have also worked with many able colleagues and I would like to mention a few: Professor John Pekruhn was the senior instructor of the course when I first came to Carnegie Mellon University. He, along with Robert Skydell, assisted during the first two years I taught and provided much needed advice. Paul Ostergaard, Raymond "Bud" Mall (some of whose photographs appear in this volume), Andrew Tesoro, and John Ritzu were important in the implementation of the exercises in the book's first and second chapters. More recently, Janice Hart, Jim Quinnan, and Barry Shields have taught freehand drawing and watercolor, and Dana Buntrock, Mark English, Bruce Lindsey, Laura Lee, Laura Nettleton, Paul Rosenblatt, and Nino Saggio have taught freehand drawing and perspective. Rebecca Schultz has provided illustrations that have appeared in both the second and third editions. Finally, my teaching assistants have been a wonderful help for me. Without their loyal support, it would be impossible to teach the course I teach.

Of all people, this book owes its greatest debt to Professor Kent Bloomer of Yale University. The assignments, criticism, and encouragement of that great educator originally led to my interest in drawing.

Introduction

INTRODUCTION

On three occasions early in his career, architect Louis I. Kahn took an extensive sketching trip in the north coastal region of Italy. Today, with the knowledge of his subsequent career in mind, it seems unmistakable that the bold and simple sense of mass and volume that so characterized his later work was first practiced here in these simple pastel and wash studies of castles and rock formations.[1]

Whenever his practice takes him to new cities for extended periods of time, Pittsburgh-based architect/urban designer Ray Gindroz always brings along a sketchbook, which he fills with contour drawings of urban spaces of every size and shape, ranging from intimate courtyards to grand piazzas. Most recently, he was in Paris and St. Petersburg. The role these sketches play in his practice is of course indirect. He is not, after all, intending to rebuild St. Petersburg of the Romanovs or fin de siecle Paris in today's world. Nevertheless, these sketches play an important role. His annotations to the drawings indicate as much. These notes point out how the architecture in each scene articulates such concepts as levels of privacy, way-finding, intimacy, grandeur, and others, important concerns for an urban designer of any age. With his sketches, Ray seems to be creating a self-renewable primer of sorts on the ways and means of urban design.

The young German architect Thomas Spiegelhalter acknowledges a course he took

Figure I.1 Louis Isidore Kahn (American, 1901–74) *Towers, San Gimignano,* 1929. Watercolor and red pencil on paper. Williams College Museum of Art. Museum purchase with funds provided by an anonymous donor and with the J. W. Field Fund, John B. Turner '24 Memorial Fund, Joseph O. Eaton Fund, Karl E. Weston Memorial Fund, Bentley W. Warren Fund 94-14.

Figure I.2 Louis I. Kahn, Alfred Newton Richards Medical Research Building, University of Pennsylvania, Philadelphia, PA, 1957–61, Louis I. Kahn Collection, University of Pennsylvania and the Pennsylvania Historical and Museum Commission.

in classical anatomy, with its emphasis on the unified structure of the skeleton and muscle groups, as one of the key experiences in the way he now thinks about the structure of buildings. Le Corbusier based his modular system on the measure of the human body.

Using the natural and man-made world as a source for the inspiration and order of design is nothing new. The sketchbooks of Leonardo da Vinci alternate so seamlessly between drawings of real objects and proposals for visionary constructions that the conclusion that one was exercise for the other is inescapable.

This book prepares students of architecture and design for the kind of drawing de-

Figure I.3 Raymond Gindroz, Urban Design Associates.

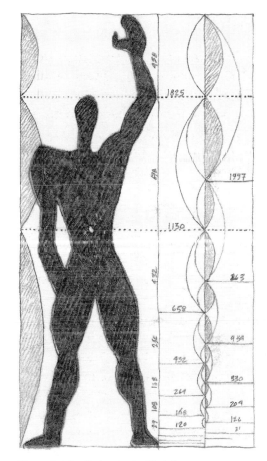

Figure I.4 Le Corbusier, *Le Modular.*

scribed above. The subject is life-drawing. The relationship of this subject to the actual practice of an architect or designer is implicit, though indirect. This book is not about drawing media, though several are practiced, and I expect students will gain considerable skill in these media in doing the exercises in this book. This is not a book about what is called "design drawing," though I anticipate that young designers and architects using this book will also (as they should) use the techniques it presents for their developmental and presentational sketches. Underlying this book is an assumption, true I believe throughout the ages: that through closer observation and understanding of the real physical world, designers come to a closer understanding of the elements of design.

[1] *The Travel Sketches* of Louis I. Kahn (Pennsylvania Academy of the Fine Arts, Philadelphia, 1978).

A PROSCRIPTIVE APPROACH BASED ON PERCEPTUAL THEORY

My approach to the subject of life-drawing owes much to the context of Carnegie Mellon's School of Architecture, where I teach, and the diversity and number of my students. Many, usually more than a third, have never had a prior course in freehand drawing. Others, likewise around a third, arrive with a rich background of museum and high school courses in studio art. Up to one-tenth of my students come from other disciplines, and my classes are large. With two or three teaching assistants (TAs), I routinely teach studio drawing to 90 first-year and 70 second-year students.

In effect, I've had to be two teachers at once and, owing to the class size, very clear about mechanics. For the beginners my approach has been quite proscriptive. I use a format of short exercises with delimited objectives and drawing materials. Simultaneously, for the more advanced students, and with a view toward a lifetime in practice, I present these exercises within a framework of perceptual theory.

Each of the book's three chapters presents life-drawing with a specific theory of perception in mind, and each chapter's exercises presume (and illustrate with drawings by the students) the understanding of vision that is specific to each theory. Taken alone, any of these approaches would be insufficient for understanding drawing, but I take them on one at a time for these reasons: 1) They sharpen focus and simplify the task of learning to draw. However simplistic each background theory might be, having to think about only one premise and implicit objective at a time makes progress easier; 2) when drawings have a specific and understandable premise, criticism of the work is more objective and therefore more helpful.

Chapter 1: Engaging the Visual World

The first chapter focuses on interaction with the environment as the key issue for drawing. It asserts that drawing is above all an active, kinesthetic, and tactile process. The hand moves. Marks are made on the paper. The focus is more on the act itself—making marks and interacting with what is drawn—and less on what the viewer brings to the process or on the nature of what is drawn.

I relate this point of view to the *transactionalist* view of perception,[2] but I credit drawing teacher Kimon Nicholaides for this understanding. Initially, with the figure and then with buildings, I have adapted most of the exercises of Chapter 1 from his superb text, *The Natural Way to Draw*.[3]

I find Nicholaides' understanding of drawing absolutely appropriate for the task that architects and designers ultimately confront. Architects and designers must create objects that do not yet exist. They make things. Appropriate to the task of making things, Nicholaides conceived of drawings as physical analogues for what is being represented. To go a step further, he considered drawing itself to be an act of *making*. He believed that pictures should not be mere imitations of what is represented, but real in themselves.

Chapter 2: The Appearance of the Visual World

The second chapter shifts away from consideration of the act of drawing and focuses on the nature of what is being drawn: the three-dimensional world. It is based on the early work of the perceptual psychologist James J. Gibson, the originator of the so-called *ecological* view of perception. Because it is central to his understanding that sensation is already ordered in itself, Gibson's work is particularly useful for architects and designers who, as a matter of course, must assume the prospect of a general order. The exercises of Chapter 2 have an analytical character. They are aimed at building knowledge of the order of the visual world as it exists and understanding of drawing as a reasoned response to that order. Subjects covered in this section are surface texture, built on Gibson's understandings of textural gradient, and freehand perspective, built on his understanding of depth cues.

Chapter 3: When Order is Made

The third chapter considers what the artist brings to the process. In a reverse of Chapter 2, here order originates in the conceptions the artist might apply to the task. Drawing is understood as a process of projecting order into the world. As an example, in this chapter the environment is made to be seen in accordance with the laws of perspective—even when perspective may not seem to apply at all. Perspective drawing and the representation of light and color form the topics of this chapter, and both are approached from this proactive stance.

Appendices

The Appendices form a reference on traditional methods of projection. Appendix A presents the "magic" and "office" methods of perspective. Appendices B and C cover shade and shadow construction in isometric and orthographic projection. Each of these subjects is presented with a format of blank and completed constructions.

In Toto

With the sum of these three very distinct approaches to drawing, a student gains a complete picture of how to draw the man-made and natural world. Whatever the subject or intention, one ultimately proceeds with various proportions of these three approaches in the mix—the first chapter having been directed at the body, the second at the mind, and the third at the spirit. In that it addresses all three, it is my hope that *Drawing and Perceiving* may serve as that one book on the subject of life-drawing for architects and designers if they have only one book to buy.

---

[2] A view of perception that emphasizes the role of interaction with the environment as a basis for perception. Leading proponents of this point of view are Adelbert Ames and John Dewey.

[3] Kimon Nicholaides, *The Natural Way to Draw* (Boston: Houghton Mifflin, 1941).

Engaging the Visual World

A foundation based on the teaching
of Kimon Nicolaides

TOUCHING AND MOVING PROVIDE THE FOUNDATION

Suspicions about vision

It is an adage of hunting that "a bird in the hand is worth two in the bush." While this saying is directed at the uncertainties of marksmanship, it also hints at the limitations of vision unaided by the affirming sense of touch. Likewise, when in some blissful moment, we are wont to say, "Touch me; prove I'm not still dreaming," we do so in recognition that it is through the sense of touch that we come closest to verifying the realness of things and events. Suspicions about vision originate in the fact that, despite its obvious usefulness, vision is less essential than the sense of touch. Imagine a world without sight, and we are impressed by the prospect of the difficulty of daily life. Imagine a world without touch, and we must wonder if life would be demonstrable or even possible.

What is so useful about vision is that it provides information at a distance. After some life experience, the unfolding image of an approaching car offers sufficient warning in itself, warning that is sufficient without the confirming crunch that would result from remaining in the middle of the road. Vision allows for a certain useful detachment from life, at more than arm's length and out of harm's way. But it is precisely for this capacity that we must consider vision as a kind of sur-

rogate sense, one step removed from the "nitty-gritty" of real life.

The fact that vision alone provides a somewhat detached sense of reality was made obvious by the televised reporting of the 1991 war in the Persian Gulf and more recently in Serbia. I refer here to those chilling (and riveting) videos that tracked "smart bombs" to their targets. So complete was our detachment that, as we watched, we also lost any sense of the human beings there at the target and the pain and suffering inflicted upon them. The all-too-droll voice-over commentary of the newscasters said as much. From the comfort of the living room, our perception remained confined to the visible, out of touch and free of pain.

If only because it is so easily deceived, there is ample cause to distrust the primacy of vision. Camouflage in warfare, trompe l'oeil in painting, and cinematic special effects are all examples of the relative ease with which the eye can be fooled.

Some perceptual psychologists, in particular the *transactionalists*,[1] believe that touch and movement play key supportive roles for vision. They believe that all perception, most particularly vision, is learned through a process of interaction (transaction) with the environment. In their view the baby learns to see by verifying the visual field through much kicking, grasping, and crawling about; a baseball player learns to see and hit a curve ball

by much swinging (and missing); and a drawing student learns to see the world in perspective first by making lines converge to common vanishing points.

Vision Insufficient for Drawing

If vision by itself is insufficient for the perceptions of daily life, is it equally suspect as a foundation for learning to draw? My own doubts about its role originated years ago in a review I was conducting of the early results of the course featured in this book. After three years of teaching drawing to students of architecture, I felt I had seen a broad enough sample of their subsequent work to be able to judge the overall direction of the course. The results had been mixed. Many of my former students had been able to use their drawing ability as a design tool in subsequent studios. But others, including some who during my drawing course had seemed to draw well, had experienced difficulty in transferring these abilities. Their drawings showed problems across the full range of the design process, and their early generational drawings were particularly weak.

By chance, at the time of my review, I was reading a book about drawing, *The Natural Way to Draw*, by Kimon Nicholaides.[2] Reading his book gave me a sudden insight into my students' problems. Earlier, I had observed that the drawings of those who had subsequent difficulty had lacked a quality evident in the drawings of those who had not: their drawings seemed inactive and purely visual. Those of their more successful colleagues, though often less skillful, seemed gestural, rough, and tactile by comparison. It occurred to me that a focus on the purely visual aspects of drawing, at the expense of a kinesthetic and tactile foundation, might contribute to a subsequent inability to use drawing effectively as a design tool.

Much of what Nicholaides wrote in introducing his exercises seemed to indicate a distrust of vision. I even got the impression that he considered vision unaided by the sense of touch to be almost voyeuristic in its detachment.

Suitability for Architects and Designers

Nicholaides' exercises require intense physical involvement with subjects. Usually, he frames the act of drawing in a way that is analogous to touching. When students draw contours, for example, they begin by imagining that their pencil is actually touching the surface of the figure. When they model surfaces, they begin by imagining that their charcoal is actually manipulating that surface.

For its relationship to design, the mass exercise is particularly interesting (see pg. 36). Before modeling the surface of the figure, Nicholaides asks students first to build the figure's mass. To do this, they have to think of the charcoal as equivalent to a real material. They start at the core of the figure and build out, mark upon mark about that core until they reach the outer surface. Then after having, in effect, already built the figure, they model its surface. In the end, these drawings acquire a heavy character that has little visual equivalence to the appearance of the person they represent. They do not in fact look like these people at all. But they are *made* like them, and this attribute points to the reason why Nicholaides' exercises are so well suited to the task that architects and designers face.

Architects and designers must design something that does not yet exist. Whereas the work of a painter might legitimately remain focused on the reception and interpretation of sensation from the visual world,[3] that of the architect and designer must be directed squarely at the task of constructing something that does not yet exist.

Consistent with this aim, this exercise (and, to a less obvious degree, the others as well) presents the act of drawing as an act of making a thing, rather than just viewing that thing. And as Nicholaides sets it up, making precedes viewing. Before we can model a figure, we have to first make it exist on the page. For the architect or designer faced with the task of designing something that does not yet exist, no other approach makes sense. If trained to draw only that which is already visible, how could they begin to draw when nothing is yet there to draw? What first marks could they make?

The next fall after my review, I adapted many of Nicholaides' exercises for my course, and I have used them ever since as its foundation. I have found it is a good strategy to introduce the exercises, as Nicholaides did, using the figure. Figure-drawing sessions have a matchless intensity and focus that makes for a good beginning. Then we apply each exercise to architectural subjects. Like the figure-drawing exercises of Nicholaides that precede them, these exercises build architectural drawing on a firm foundation. When we draw, we do not just imitate an object's appearance. On the page before us, we consider each drawing to be real in itself. That is Nicholaides great gift.

---

[1] Principal advocates of this position are Adelbert Ames and John Dewey.

[2] Kimon Nicholaides, *The Natural Way to Draw* (Boston: Houghton Mifflin, 1941).

[3] Impressionism would be an example.

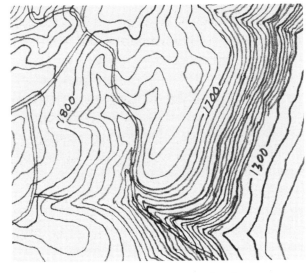

Figure 1.1 Nicholaides' interest originated with contour maps.

NICHOLAIDES AND CONTOUR

Movement Is the Basis of Contour

Nicholaides' interest in contour as a fundamental issue for drawing grew out of his work with the Camouflage Corps in the military service in France during World War I. As part of his job, he had to study contour maps, and he grew fascinated with the rich and readable sense of the landscape encoded in this abstraction. Later he incorporated the issue into his teaching at the Art Students' League in New York. Indeed, contour became so central to his conception of drawing that it was the subject with which he opened his book, *The Natural Way to Draw.*

Figure 1.2 The roadway's twisting contour sharpened my friends' perception of the altitude and drop-off.

For me, the subject of contour has always been linked with the experience of moving across the landscape. Last summer, some friends of mine told me about a drive they took over the Furka Pass in Switzerland. It is a torturous sequence of switch-backs and steep grades. Just as they got over the summit to begin their descent, and upon seeing the view before them, everyone in the car suddenly stopped talking. Snaking down the slope and shining in the sunlight, the road dropped down into the valley—with no guardrail. Without that rail, the twisting contour down the slope so sharpened their sense check the fineness of silk garments, we run our fingers over them. In the end, it is actual movement—and movement alone—that delivers the verification.

Knowing Contours from Afar

However, though real physical movement does underlie our understanding, once we've learned to interpret them, visual contours do provide sufficient information about surfaces without our ever having to actually touch them or cross them. In effect, they offer the experience of movement, but from afar. That is vision's great gift.

For someone on shore observing a boat on a smooth lake or a canoe on whitewater rapids, the contours of each scene are sufficient in themselves for understanding. The gentle waves and unbroken reflection of the rowboat in the first instance and the turbulent water and canoe all akimbo in the second instance provide enough information already. We don't need to get in the boat and paddle or get wet to know the character of each experience.

And so it was with my friends on the Furka Pass. They could "feel" the steepness from the visual contours of the road alone. They felt fear from the top of the pass, even before they began their descent.

Figure 1.3 For an observer on shore, the contours alone are sufficient for understanding. (based on *Canoe on the Rapids* by Winslow Homer).

of the altitude and sheer drop-off that what had been a nice summer's drive became a white-knuckle descent.

Notwithstanding my friends' fears, I offer the following qualification: *Ultimately, the only real basis for establishing the form of a surface is actually moving on that surface.* How does a skater really find out if the ice on a pond is smooth?—by skating on it. How did Magellan's crew finally establish that the Earth is round?—by sailing around it. The proof is in the moving.

We establish even the most subtle qualities of surfaces by moving across them. To

Figure 1.4 S. Maria del Fiore, Florence (Photo: Howard Saalman).

Figure 1.5 Side chapels, Orvieto.

Figure 1.6 Composite columns, Siena (Photo: Howard Saalman).

Knowing Surface from Afar

The material properties of surfaces offer a similar kind of information: touch and movement from afar. This is particularly the case with objects that have a good deal of surface texture. Years ago, I spent six months living in Tuscany, and in nearly every town of the province I found churches striped with alternating courses of black and white marble. One reason for the stripes is to signify use. In Tuscany, only religious buildings have stripes; secular buildings have none. But I was also struck by the extent to which these stripes seemed to articulate form. All these churches have very readable forms. This is the case whether we are considering whole structures, such as Brunelleschi's octagonal cupola in Florence, building parts such as the apsidal side chapels at Orvieto, or details such as the composite columns at Siena. The stripes make these forms graphically apparent.

The same is true of more mundane objects as well, whether natural or artificial. We perceive the shape of the neck of the wart hog in Figure 1.7 on the basis of the curving pattern of creases on its skin; similarly, we perceive the roundness of the basket in Figure 1.8 on the basis of its pattern of woven reeds. Though touching these objects would surely enrich our understanding, we do not ab-

Figure 1.7 Neck of a warthog (Photo: Raymond Mall).

Figure 1.8 Basket made of reeds.

Figure 1.9 Legs with fishnet stockings (Photo: R. Mall).

solutely need to touch them to know that they are round. The eye learns to follow the paths the hand once travelled.

Sometimes, objects lack sufficient contour or surface texture to be easily perceived. In such instances, we sometimes augment or exaggerate their material properties to make their form more apparent. This practice, evident in the striped churches of Tuscany, lies at the heart of decoration. Chrome stripes on a

1950s car and fishnet stockings on a Las Vegas showgirl are each in their own way intended to add contour to surfaces.

Figure 1.10 A 1953 Buick Skylark (Photo: Sarah Cooper).

Surface Contour and Building Elevations

Knowledge of material contours becomes a key issue for the design of building elevations. In the example of Enric Miralles' cemetery in Ingualada, Spain, the precast concrete shelves that line the ascending walkway articulate the walkway's rise by providing contours that also step up.

But articulation of shape and surface form are not the only issues that arise with contour. The orientation of occupants, indeed their sense of stability, can be at stake. Frank Gehry's fabulous Guggenheim Museum in Bilbao, Spain, is a good instance to point to. The environment visitors walk through is complex. The forms are not rectangular. The shapes are not familiar. A queasy, ill-at-ease sensation could easily have been the result had Gehry not carefully kept the horizontal material contours plainly visible so that a readable sense of the forms of the surfaces is evident.

The Contour Exercises

Through their instructions, the exercises that follow will retrace the line of thought presented so far. In the spirit of verifying the visual field kinesthetically at the outset, they will begin with touch and movement and only then will turn to vision alone. To deepen your understanding of the primacy of real physical movement as the basis for vision, every effort will be made to heighten your awareness of movement while you draw. I will ask that you

Figure 1.11 Cemetery, Enric Miralles, Igualada, Spain (Photo: Bruce Lindsey).

be attentive to the motion of your hand and eyes while you draw. I will ask that you move slowly and deliberately at the start. Later, I will ask you to consciously vary your speed. We will use the act of drawing—the act of looking at a scene and making marks in imi-

tation of that scene—as the point of departure for your understanding. In the end, by imitating the contours of buildings, you will come to understand how the the material facts of the built world around us can manifest themselves to us through contours and,

Figure 1.12a Guggenheim Museum, Bilbao, Spain. Frank Gehry (Photo: Bruce Lindsey).

Figure 1.12b Guggenheim Museum, Bilbao, Spain. Frank Gehry (Photo: Bruce Lindsey).

Figure 1.13 You get good at sports when your touch and vision are in sync.

thus, through vision alone — how "seeing can be believing."

Comparisons between drawing and sport are often helpful. Some of you have learned to perform amazing athletic feats quite well. You have learned to hit baseballs and tennis balls, and sink jump-shots. Your abilities have been built on a kinesthetic foundation of touching and moving in addition to looking. And you have routinely had to practice these athletic skills over and over and over again to get them right. You became good at them only when your touch and movement and vision were all in sync with each other. Your ability to draw should have a foundation that is no less firm.

CONTOUR 1

Follow your eyes, and don't peek.

Felt-tipped pen, bond paper

With the intention of introducing touch and movement as the basis for drawing, the first two exercises ask you to draw without looking at the drawing while you're doing it.

Begin by looking at some point along the contour of the model and, at the same time, imagine that your pen on the page is actually touching that same point on the model. Let your eyes move slowly along the contour of the model. Then, without looking at your drawing, and in one continuous line, let your pen follow the movement of your eyes as they follow the contour over and across the surface of the model. Draw very deliberately and very slowly. Resist the temptation of looking at the page. Keep the conviction that your pen is in fact touching the model.

Consciously follow contours across the form as well as along it. Be inventive. Follow contours such as edges of shadows and creases in the skin, in short anything that will take you away from the outside edge.[4]

Figure 1.14 Cynthia Sandling Macshane.

Comments: *A spirit of pure joy in movement should compel these drawings. Don't expect them to result in a likeness. When you're done and finally do look at them, laugh about the distortions!*

[4] Adapted from "Contour," in Kimon Nicholaides, *The Natural Way to Draw*, pp. 9–14.

Figure 1.15 Jo Frost.

CONTOUR 2

Draw an interior and, again, don't peek.

Felt-tipped pen, bond paper

Find an interior space with a set of interesting contours. The space should have overlapping elements such as furniture, columns, beams, arches, and ceiling lights. Church interiors are usually a good choice.

Look at some point along the surface contours of this space and, at the same time, imagine that your pen on the page is actually touching that point at which you are looking.

Still without looking at your drawing, let your eyes move slowly along the contour. Still in one continuous line, let your pen follow the movement of your eyes as they follow the contour around the space.

Do let your eye and hand jump from foreground to background elements. Draw deliberately and very slowly. Resist the temptation to look at the page. Keep the conviction that your pen is actually touching the surface of the space.[5]

Comments: *When you don't allow yourself to look at the drawing in progress (and even when you do), contour drawing is an incremental process. By not looking, you remove the governance of vision over holistic issues of shape and proportion, and a more playful line results. Welcome this prospect and retain it.*

I compare the mood of contour drawing to a relaxed summer drive through the countryside when you have no exact destination and no appointments to keep. You turn off main roads. You follow small lanes. Whimsy and spontaneity guide you. Similar moods should guide your line-work in this and subsequent exercises.

[5] *Ibid.*

CONTOUR 3

Now and then glance at the page.

Felt-tipped pen, bond paper

Draw the contour of the model as you did in exercise 1, but this time allow yourself an occasional glance at the drawing. Maintain the sense that your pen is touching the surface of the model as it moves along the contour of the model.

In this exercise, vary the pace at which you move on the page. Areas with more detail or more interesting shapes should cause your eyes to linger. Other areas will let you speed quickly over them. Your line-work should reflect these distinctions.

After you have completed several drawings, add a spatial dimension to your work by including objects in the foreground or background. You might draw one of your colleagues across the room or an architectural element. Note the differences among projected sizes: the greater area occupied by objects in the foreground and the smaller area of those in the background. Note how much richer your sense of depth becomes when a foreground is articulated by near objects.[6]

_____

[6] *Ibid.*

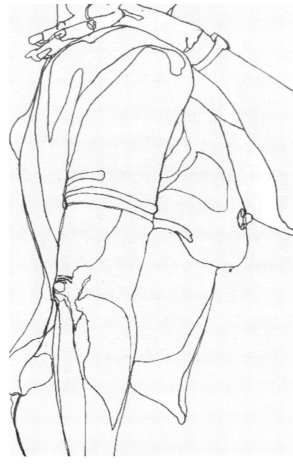

Figure 1.16 Jonathan Kline.

Figure 1.17 Jonathan Kline.

Comments: *Having the model wear some articles of clothing helps to vary the pace of lines. Clothing also makes cross-contours on the model somewhat easier to find. The armlet the model is wearing in Figure 1.16 is one such instance. The spatial dimension that immediately arises when both foreground and background are included can be startling. Your picture suddenly seems like a view!*

Figure 1.18 Erin Nunes.

Figure 1.19 Brent Capron.

Dip your stick into the India ink and draw the contour of the model as you did in exercise 1, but this time actively vary the width of the line. Roll the stick in your fingers and roll your wrist as you draw. Let the line get thick and dark along some contours that seem more expressive or important. Then let it get thin and even vanish altogether at other places.[7]

Comments: *This is absolutely an exercise that you learn by doing. You will not feel in control at the start. Don't try to be. Give your hand and arm time to master the unpredictability of the medium on their own.*

As you proceed, notice how varying the line-weight can express formal properties in your subject. In Figure 1.18, the fleeting line on the hip expresses its bulge. In Figure 1.19, heavier lines on the columns express the fact that they overlap the background.

CONTOUR 4

Vary the width of the line.

A chewed-off stick, india ink, bond paper

At this point we start to vary the tools. Find an old stick of wood. It can be about 6 inches long and maybe a quarter-inch in diameter. Cut off the end so that a quill-like edge somewhat like that of a calligraphy pen is the result.

---

[7] *Ibid.*

CONTOUR 5

Vary the character of the line.

Conté crayon, newsprint

Once again we're going to change materials and exploit the possibilities of a new material: conté crayon. With conté you can vary the pressure to make lines darker and lighter. By rolling the conté in your fingers as you draw, you can also change the line width. It can be pointed if you use a corner, wider if you use a full edge, and wider still if you use an entire side. Take advantage of these possibilities to express varying levels of importance among contours. Some may carry a greater sense of the form. Others, such as overlapping edges, may record important spatial relationships. In a playful manner, always in a playful manner, give these lines greater weights.[8]

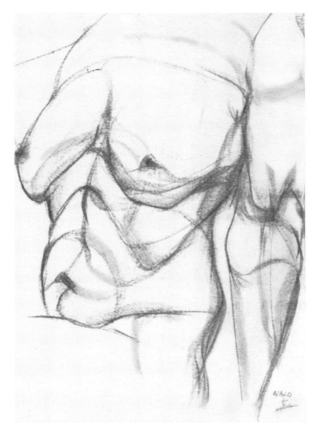

Figure 1.20 Najd Hanna.

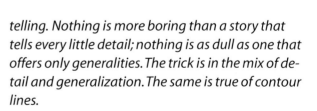

Figure 1.21 Jonathan Kline.

Comments: *Because both are linear in time, I like to compare drawing contour lines to storytelling. Good storytellers know to vary the pace and level of detail. At times, they offer quick generalizations to set a context; at other times, they hone in on the most precise descriptions of salient features or events. Unevenness is at the heart of good storytelling. Nothing is more boring than a story that tells every little detail; nothing is as dull as one that offers only generalities. The trick is in the mix of detail and generalization. The same is true of contour lines.*

---

[8] *Ibid.*

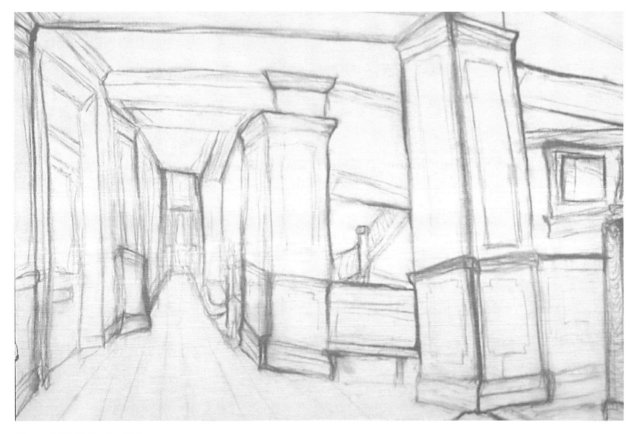

Figure 1.22 Katherine Bojsza.

The choice of what you draw is important. Pick an interior or exterior site that has parallel lines, numerous corners, and a fair degree of height. Pick a subject with a variety of shapes and concentrations of detail. Don't sit too far away from what you are drawing. Too great a distance will lessen the inclinations of the horizontal lines in your subject.

Above all, pick a scene that has significant overlaps and that seems to articulate a sense of foreground with these overlaps. To be called views, all views must have foregrounds. Pick one that has one![9]

Comments: *Vision is an uneven sense. We do not see all things equally. Nor do we see all things at the same time. If we did, we would have simply too much information to process. Instead, we attend only to some things. Our eyes scan the visual field restlessly, searching out that information and those attributes that are pertinent. We ignore the rest.*

In the spirit of the above, I like to address the uneven levels of detail that seeing and drawing a building entails by invoking Mohammed Ali's famous advice: "Float like a butterfly, sting like a bee." Let your line float like a butterfly when the information is simple and unchanging, and sting like a bee when it seems pertinent and grabs your attention.

CONTOUR 6

Draw contours in perspective.

Conté crayon, newsprint

Now is the right time to begin trying to record linear perspective. It is not at all necessary to think about constructing parallel lines to common vanishing points or registering foreshortening. On the contrary, these more intellectual understandings would be counterproductive at this time. Rather, you should focus on feeling the inclination that perspective contours take as you follow them with your eye and hand.

---

[9] *Ibid.*

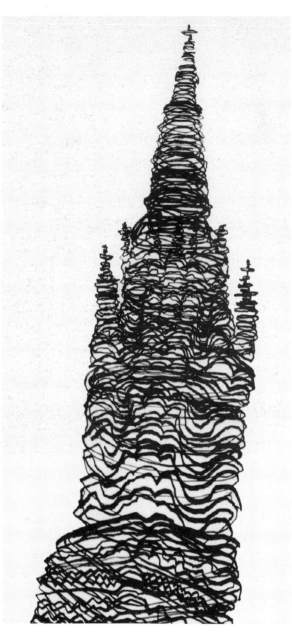

Figure 1.23 Paul Shea.

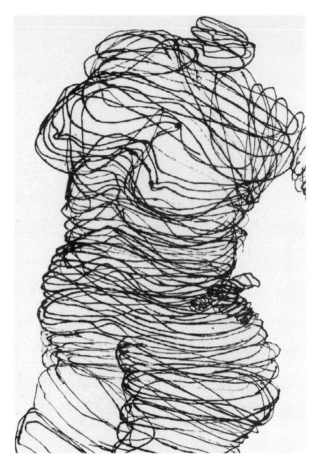

Figure 1.24 R. James Pett.

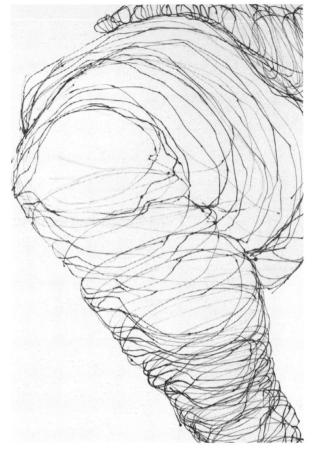

Figure 1.25 Marybeth Barrett.

CONTOUR 7
Wrap the form.

Felt-tipped pen to begin, then conté

This exercise extends your sense of cross-contour, lines that move across and around forms. Because it goes all the way around forms, much like contour maps, this exercise comes closest to the circumstance that piqued Nicholaides' interest in contour in the first place.

Begin by looking at some point on the edge of the model where the cross-contour seems readable. The waistline or the shoulders are usually good choices. Convince yourself that your pen is touching that point. Starting there, imagine you would wrap a ball of string across the front and around the back of the model. Draw that string and keep drawing that string around and around the model.

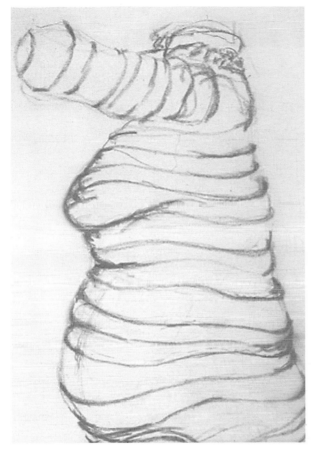

Figure 1.26 William Merriman.

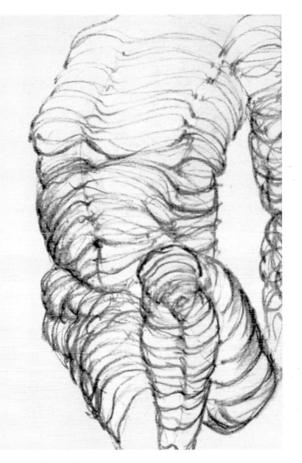

Figure 1.27 Najd Hanna.

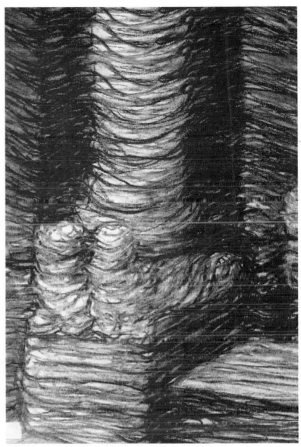

Figure 1.28 Rebecca Schultz.

After a while, switch to conté and to showing just the visible side. But as you leave out the backside, do not lose your sense of its shape. Hook the line just slightly behind the model when it reaches the outside edge. Lines should seem to embrace the form.[10]

Comments: *The model's pose for this exercise is key. A pose with the shoulders rotated away from the angle of the waist usually makes the cross con-*

tours more readable. Where you sit to draw the pose is also important. For a standing pose, sit close and low to the ground and look up at an angle. You want the sectional properties of the cross-contours to be as open as possible to your view.

In an effort to make the spatial orientation of the cross-contours more readable, draw a line down the center of the stomach or draw the spine. These lines help you establish the twist and pos-

ture of the model and thereby clarify the shape of each cross-contour. This exercise is not easy and there is always a tendency to oversimplify the shapes. You need to avoid making Michelin men!

---

[10] Adapted from "Cross Contours," in Kimon Nicholaides, *The Natural Way to Draw*, pp. 20–22.

Figure 1.29 Derek Schmidt.

Figure 1.30 Jarrett Pelletier.

Figure 1.31 Edward Pak.

CONTOUR 8

Draw the figure with straight lines only.

Conté crayon, newsprint

This exercise is an intermediate step between drawing contours and starting to sense and record convergence in the visual field: the heart of perspective drawing.

Approach drawing the figure as you have in previous contour exercises, but this time limit yourself to straight lines only. No curving lines are allowed!

Comments: *Stand up for this exercise and hold the conté between your thumb and forefinger. Keep your wrist somewhat stiff while you draw. By holding the conté in this manner, you will be*

forced to make a kind of slashing motion with your whole arm as you make the individual straight lines. Drawing with your whole arm is to be welcomed. It will help you sense the directionality of the marks as you make them.

Figure 1.32 Brian Leet.

Figure 1.33 Brian Leet.

CONTOUR 9
Sense and imitate convergence.

Conté crayon, newsprint

This exercise concludes a sequence that began with following contours and that now ends with perspective drawing. In this last exercise, our purpose is not to construct perspectives; it is to sense convergence and then imitate it. We are trying to derive perspective as a fact of the visual field and feel it with our hands and arms as we do so.

Find an architectural scene with numerous corners and a strong and well-articulated foreground. It should be one you can draw from above (or below), at a steep angle. A view from a mezzanine or a stairway with strongly stated banisters and newel-posts is ideal.

Use the same sort of slashing mark you used in the previous exercise. The slashing motion you make with your whole arm as you draw is intended to exaggerate your imitation of convergence. Exaggeration in general is good: whether of steepness, breadth of field, or convergence.

Figure 1.34 Bruce Pollock.

Figure 1.35 Vincent Chew.

Figure 1.36 Vincent Chew.

Comments: *Pittsburgh is an environment rich with roadways, houses, and city steps set on steep slopes, ideal conditions for this exercise. But if your environment lacks these, use slides as an alternative. Pick scenes where the convergence is obvious from the angle of the view. Use sites that are sufficiently steep, and always exaggerate that steepness.*

This exercise was the key for Missi, who was having great difficulty reading perspective convergences above the horizon line. Above the horizon line, lines descend as they move away from the *viewer, the opposite of what occurs below the horizon line. Missi just couldn't grasp this fact; that is, she could understand it, but she couldn't incorporate it into the way she drew. Then she did the drawing shown in Figure 1.37 and I noticed a sudden change in her work. It was as if this technique and the view she chose, with the convex shape of the circular roof overhead, brought this issue home for her.*

Figure 1.37 Missi Nickle.

Figure 1.38 View 1.

Figure 1.39 View 2.

Figure 1.40 View 3.

CONTOUR AND COMPOSITION

Detachment and Composition

With respect to the basics of contour views—how to think about them, how to make them—Nicholaides has written much. But what about their composition? He has written little on that subject. Because composition has important implications for architectural design, we need to address it before moving on.

A good place to start is where we began: with Nicholaides' deep distrust of vision and his sense that drawings gain strength when they are built on the basis of touch rather than on vision alone. Earlier, I suggested that what is so suspicious about vision is its detachment: *we are here, and we are looking there, but we are not part of the situation at which we are looking.* While this separation is precisely what is so useful about vision—the

person sighting a mortar and lobbing shells does not, after all, want to be where the bombs land—it is separation nonetheless. And Nicholaides distrusted drawing for that reason alone.

Almost in an effort to salve Nicholaides' concerns about the drawings we make, we might ask: How could we compose views in a way to lessen his sense that we are detached from what we are drawing?

For a start, I offer a comparison of the three views presented in Figures 1.38, 1.39, and 1.40. All of them show the same object, but the sense we get of the relationship of observer to object differs among them. The first shows a clear connection between the observer and object: an arm is holding it. The second is more ambiguous: the object is just *there*, and we have little sense where the observer is. The third is more clear about location—the observer is in a room separated from the object by the wall—but the connection of observer to object, though implied, remains unclear.

If, from among these three views, we had to choose one that would come closest to establishing a sense of connection between observer and object, what Nicholaides wants, then we would surely have to pick the first, where the connection is direct and physical. But that selection would also suggest that we should compose only views in which the observer is touching or nearly touching the objects in a scene. Is there another way?

Making Views Touch

What if we were to add some elements to the third view, elements that would make it more like the first view, but not show an arm and a hand? We might, for example, add a wing to the building to show that the observer is on the second floor. Likewise, we might construct that wing to overlap parts of the object and

Figure 1.41 View 4.

thereby clarify its location without depicting an actual observer.

We should understand the significance of these additions for the kinesthetic and tactile way in which Nicholaides frames his entire approach to drawing. While it is true that the hand is no longer actually touching the object in Figure 1.41, the eye is still able to touch it by extension. In a way that the hand and body might follow—across the roof and down the column—the eye is still able to reach the object. The view's composition establishes the path.

Figure 1.42 Brad Jencks.

Figure 1.43 Jarek Babicki.

A Law for Good Composition

We might therefore state as almost a law of good composition that:

1) Every view must have a foreground—the position of the observer must be in some way represented.

2) Every view must have a route for the eye to travel—the connection of foreground to middle and background must be clear.

3) Every view must have a destination—a place the eye can go to.

Delight

And what about delight? Surely there is more to composition than just establishing foreground, middleground, and background.

There is in New Mexico a wonderful tradition at Christmastime. To light the way for the the three kings to come visit the newborn

Figure 1.44 Mark Siwek.

Figure 1.45 Patricia Clark.

Christchild, *luminarias*; candles in small translucent bags, are laid out every few yards along both sides of the roads across the barren desert landscape. And in the cool winter night, as one looks out from each promontory, one feels a rare connection with the surroundings. From foreground to background, the eye is led by these candle-lighted contours, point by point, out across the landscape and into every town.

This is vision made connected place to place, from foreground to object, in a way that would not merely satisfy Nicholaides but delight him as well. Compose your views thusly.

Connect the observer to the world out there with an equal sense of magic!

Some Well–Composed views

Taking the implication that well-composed views shall have well defined foregrounds and paths for the eyes, here are some examples—with their visual paths laid out.

Frank Lloyd Wright and Composition

Among modern architects, Frank Lloyd Wright provides some of the best examples of the rule that well-composed views shall have well-defined foregrounds and delightful paths for the eyes to follow. Wright was a master of zigzag, two-point perspective paths into the background.

Figures 1.46 and 1.47 show Fallingwater, Wright's masterpiece near Pittsburgh. In Figure 1.46, the foreground is the bridge, and the zigzag path of the cantilevers leads the eye up into the woods or alternatively to the falls. In Figure 1.47, the foreground is the rocks and the falls themselves; the overhanging terraces lead the eye on up the hill.

Figure 1.46 Fallingwater: view across the bridge.

Figure 1.47 Fallingwater, drawing after rendering by Frank Lloyd Wright.

NICHOLAIDES AND MASS

Suspicions about Appearance

In introducing the subject of *mass* in *The Natural Way to Draw*, Nicholaides decries a certain shallow and superficial sense of form that characterizes some drawings. To him, these drawings miss essential properties of objects; he points to instances of "cast-iron clouds" and "balloonlike women" as examples. He goes on to explain that our first, most real sensation of most objects is of their "weight," something that we usually gain by actually holding or hefting them. And almost as if we are engaged in just that, holding or hefting objects, he suggests that we should start a drawing by representing the weight of our subject. In this Nicholaides reveals a preference for the material properties of objects and a distrust of their appearances. What lies behind his suspicion about appearance?

Background of Nicholaides' Suspicions

Nicholaides was not the first to raise the issue. In the history of Western art there is a long-running debate about the question of reality versus appearance, and much of that debate casts doubt on the value of two-dimensional images. In "The Republic," Plato dismisses the work of painters as lowlier even than that of common furnituremakers. Plato considered working with concepts to be the highest and most real activity. To the extent they depended upon the senses, he distrusted all other activities. But in this passage he showed particular contempt for painters. Even the furnituremaker, Plato allowed, is at least making a real object—an instance of a concept and thus only one step removed. But as for the painter, not only does he work with an object, he limits himself to the appearance of a single aspect of it.[11]

Reading his words in "The Republic," we even get the impression that Plato believes there is something truly sinful about painting (in one instance, he characterizes painters as deceivers of children).[12] But if we accept Plato on faith, even acknowledging that dealing with appearances is somehow suspect, how might we nudge painting and drawing a notch or two higher in Plato's eyes?

Years ago in a second-grade classroom, I got into a reality versus appearance argument with my then best friend, Toby McCarthy. The two of us had made drawings of military airplanes—this was during the Korean War—and I thought mine was better. His was drawn planlike, from above; all the parts were visible, and he was busy trying out various placements for gun turrets—on the sides, on top, even on the wings. Mine was drawn in eye-level perspective from the side, with both wings foreshortened, and one wing partly obscured. In my memory, my airplane really did appear to be flying.

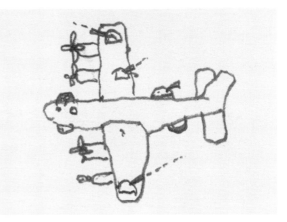

Figure 1.48 Toby's drawing.

Toby's argument was about function, and he was blunt. My plane had only one and one-half wings and one and one-half engines. His drawing might not look like an airplane in flight, but at least his *could* fly! Only his had the necessary parts. On and on the argument went from his desk at one end of the row to mine at the other.

Toby was emphasizing the "thingness" of his picture over its command of appearance. Could it be used as an airplane? Could it be flown? This is essentially the same argument as Nicholaides' with respect to mass. Although Nicholaides does not actually lay it out in this way, his comments have the same functional ring. Where Toby asked me to imagine flying my airplane (and his), Nicholaides asks us to imagine weighing our drawings.[13]

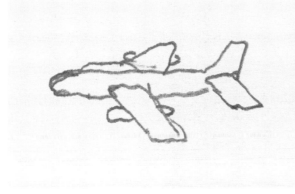

Figure 1.49 My drawing.

The more positive rating on Plato's scale, which I believe would be awarded to both Nicholaides' and Toby's interpretations, lies in their conception of a drawing as a *thing* in its own right. For both, making a drawing is more like the activity of Plato's furnituremaker: more like making an object than making an appearance. At the heart of this conception is Nicholaides' exercise on weight.

Nicholaides' Exercise on Weight

With his exercise on weight (called *mass* in this volume; see pg. 36), Nicholaides doesn't only ask us to weigh the object, he asks us to build it, too, mark by mark upon the page. Consider how he starts us off. We are to imagine that we are drawing the core of our subject. Then, much like making a snowball, we are to pack material about that core, in back,

to the sides, and in front. In the end, these drawings achieve a heavy, brooding sense of weight that does not reflect the subject's appearance at all. But though they may not look like our subject, they are *made* like it!

Nicholaides' and Toby McCarthy's drawings suggest something very different from our common understanding of the relationship of a drawing to what is represented. With the word "drawing" we often mean—I believe mistakenly—a somewhat diminished second-hand version of the thing in the picture. This is hardly an adequate description for a drawing such as Toby's. After all, how many planes have you seen lately that have turrets on their wings?

What Drawings Must Do

What then must a drawing do? What the real thing can do! But also more. It must not only be able to take the place of what it represents, it must empower us over it, too. A drawing of an airplane must allow the construction of an airplane for those Toby McCarthys of the world who are too young (or too poor) to buy the parts. A plan drawing of a building must enable an architect to build, tear down, and rebuild (with graphite and paper) the interim trial solutions that a client could not afford to build if executed in real bricks and mortar. And a drawing of mass must allow us to build and shape the material of which an object is made. These are but some of the capacities

that come naturally once we treat a drawing as "the real thing" and not a fake.

[11] Plato, "The Republic," in the *Dialogues of Plato*, translated into English by B. Jowett (New York: Random House, 1937), book X, pp. 852–879.

[12] *Ibid.*

[13] This fuctional interpretation of Toby's drawing owes to E. H. Gombrich's brilliant essay, "Meditations on a Hobby Horse," in *Aspects of Form*; Edited by L. L. Whyte (Bloomington: Indiana University Press, 1966), pp. 209–228.

MASS 1

Build mass with lithographic crayon.

Crayon, bond paper

Position the lithographic crayon at the center of the page. Imagine that the crayon is positioned at the center of gravity of the model. Build mass out from that center: behind, below, to the sides, and in front of the center. Work as if packing layers of snow onto a snowball or layers of clay onto an armature. Keep building outward until you reach the surface of the model.

When it is completed, your drawing should be dark where the model is thick and light where the model is thin.

For a version of this exercise that is a real doodler's delight, try the same exercise, but use ballpoint pen instead. Then it becomes much like the kind of drawing we often do almost mindlessly while on the phone.[14]

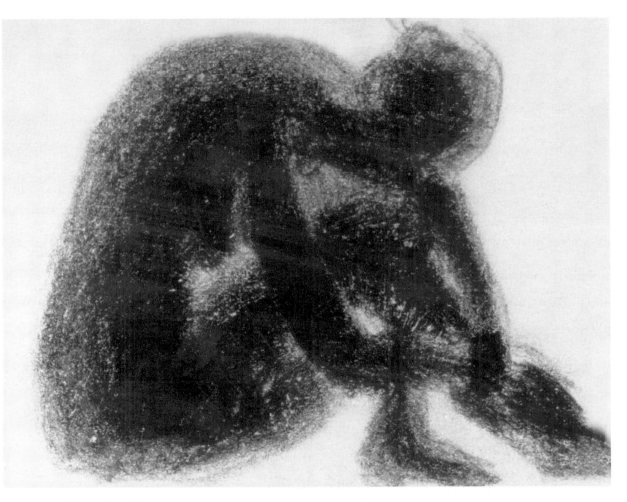

Figure 1.50 Christopher Farley.

---

14 Adapted from "Weight," in Kimon Nicholaides, *The Natural Way to Draw,* pp. 33–35.

Comments: *These drawings often take on interesting histories. At times, they even cancel themselves out by becoming too dark. Don't worry! They don't have to reach a particular degree of likeness. The value is in the sense you gain of actually making an object while you draw.*

It is interesting to note the differences that arise among these drawings. Chris (in Figure 1.50) developed his from the center out. The other two seemed to consider theirs more like clay statues. Muscles and breasts were added on by adding hunks of charcoal onto the figure.

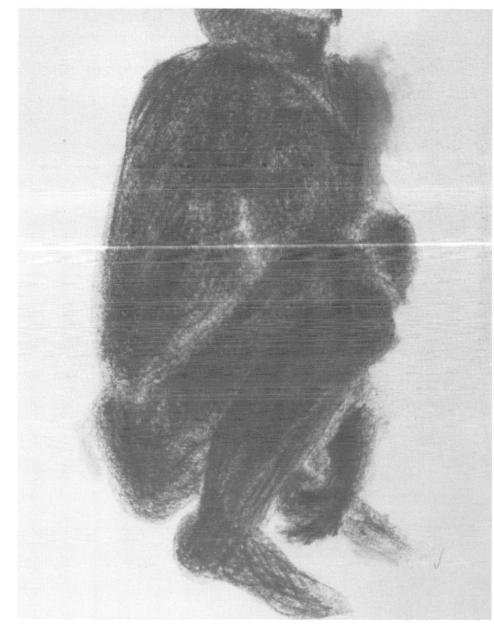

Figure 1.51 Elizabeth Freed.

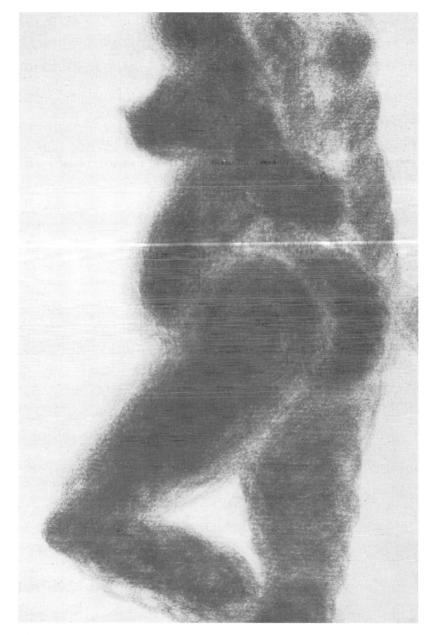

Figure 1.52 (unknown artist).

MASS 2

Model with charcoal.

Charcoal (soft black), newsprint

Lightly build out the mass of the figure with tone (as you did in exercise 1), but do this more rapidly and more softly. When you reach the surface of the figure, model that surface. Where the surface moves back away from you, press the charcoal into the page. Where the surface moves out toward you, ease the pressure on the charcoal.[15]

Comments: *What is so powerful about this exercise is the degree to which it re-creates the activity of modeling a real form. If you were working in clay, you would push into that form where you would want to depress its surface. You do the same here in this drawing; you press harder into the page with the charcoal. There is an exact mechanical correspondence between the represented act of modeling and the real act.*

Figure 1.53 Andrés Petruscak.

---

[15] Adapted from "Modeled in Litho-Crayon," in Kimon Nicholaides, *The Natural Way to Draw*, pp. 36–39.

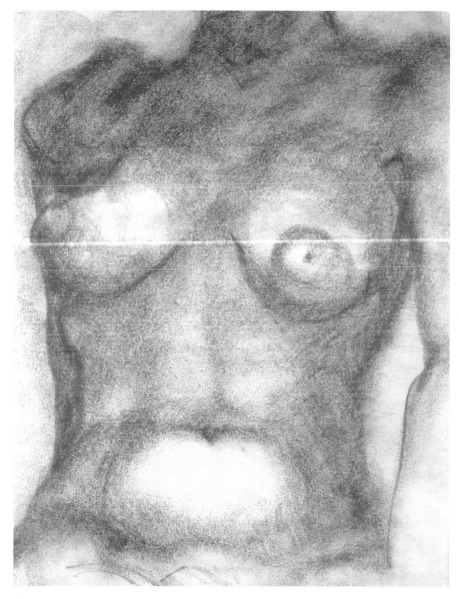

Figure 1.54 Kimberly Ruane Biagioli.

Figure 1.55 David Barger.

MASS 3

Model with ink scribble.

Felt-tipped pen, newsprint

Lightly build out the mass of the figure with ink scribble (as you did in exercises 1 and 2, but more rapidly and lightly). When you reach the surface of the figure, model that surface. Where the surface moves back away from you, scribble more; where the surface moves out toward you, scribble less.[16]

Comments: *As you do this exercise, think of shaping a plaster of paris figure with a rasp. Where you would want to depress the surface, you would file more; where you would want the form to remain as it is, you would file less.*

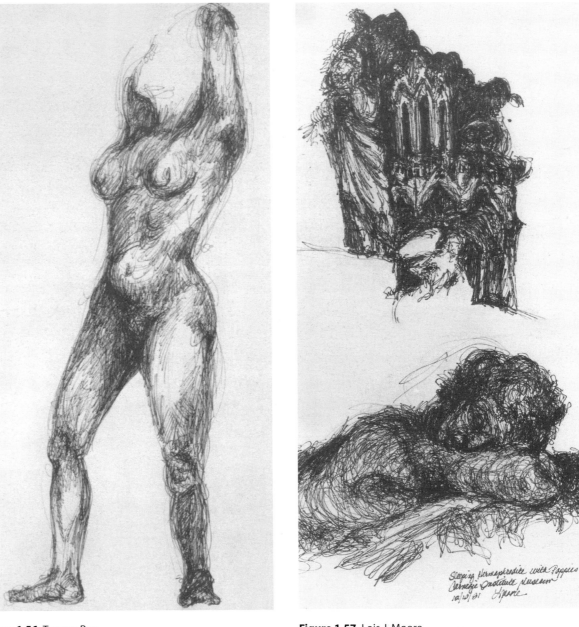

Figure 1.56 Tammy Roy.

Figure 1.57 Lois J. Moore.

[16] Adapted from "Modeled in Ink," in Kimon Nicholaides, *The Natural Way to Draw,* pp. 51–52.

Figure 1.58 Rebecca Schultz.

Figure 1.59 Paul Shea.

DRAWING AND MAKING

Implications for Design Drawings

In the previous exercises on mass, Nicholaides framed the process in such a way that we believed the marks on the page were material. We built figures outward from their cores, and we slabbed muscles over bones much as we would if we were building clay statues. How might this understanding of drawing have an impact on the drawings that architects make when they design?

Figure 1.60 shows one from a series of developmental drawings by the young German architect Thomas Spiegelhalter. He did these partly as life drawings—they started as drawings of machinery at gravel pits in Germany—and partly as exploratory drawings for proposals for works on that site.

What is important to observe in these drawings is how they are made. Much as Nicholaides' drawings of mass, these drawings have a compelling materiality. Building members are scribbled and smeared into existence, and assembled in place on the page as objects. What we see here is not detached observation, but building in process.

Later, the impact of a similar order of assembly, first recorded at the gravel pit, emerges in the house, shown in Figures 1.61 and 1.62, by Thomas at another location in Germany.

Figure 1.60 Thomas Spiegelhalter.

Figure 1.61 Thomas Spiegelhalter.

Figure 1.62 Thomas Spiegelhalter.

GESTURE

Gesture drawing is at the very heart of Nicholaides' conception of drawing. Indeed, if it is fair to describe Nicholaides' approach as one from which we learn by doing and learn by making, then with gesture drawing we go one step further: we learn by being.

The form, even of motionless objects, is a consequence of force. Their lack of motion indicates only that their present forces are counterbalanced; it does not indicate a lack of force. Attesting to our ability to perceive such forces are words we use to describe posture: "crouch," "slouch," and "lean" all describe motionless states; but they also characterize the unique muscular resolution of each stance. We see a poised cat or a coiled snake and feel an intense balance of forces despite the stillness of the animal.

The same is true of our perceptions of inanimate objects. We see a bridge across a gorge and use a word such as "leap" to describe the manner in which it spans from one side to the other.

The intent of gesture-drawing is to give form to these insights. Gesture drawing relies on empathetic sensation.[17] As we draw something, we attempt to be that thing and feel what

---

[17] Empathy is usually used to mean a capacity to share the emotional feelings of another person. It is used here by analogy to mean a capacity to share the physical sensation of another person or, by transfer, of an inanimate thing.

Figure 1.63 *Eiffel as the Tower.* After a drawing from *Punch,* 1889. Empathetic sensation is feeling the same sensation as that thing.

Figure 1.64 Overlooking the J&L Mill from Robinson & Aliquippa, *University Center Mural* (detail), by the author, 10'h × 200'w, Carnegie Mellon University (Photo: Ken Andreyo).

it is doing. If we are drawing a person who is leaning against a wall, then we try to make our lines lean as well. If we are drawing the Hoover Dam holding back Lake Mead, then we try to make our lines hold back a wall of water!

In my own drawings of Pittsburgh, I experience the issue of gesture most directly when drawing houses on the city's steep slopes. During the years of the dominance of the steel industry there, when Pittsburgh was quite literally "Hell with the lid off," workers' houses were built on the most precarious slopes—just so the workers could be near the mills. When I look at these houses today, they often seem as if at any moment they might let hold and slide down the hill. So when I draw them, I draw them all akimbo. And I draw them so that they seem to be leaning back into the hill to resist the slide, much as I would in the same place!

GESTURE 1

Feel and draw what the model is doing.

Crayon or charcoal, newsprint

The model will take a series of quick, active poses that will last less than a minute. As the model holds a pose, let your crayon sweep freely and continuously around the paper. Move it rapidly and let it be driven by a sense of the forces present in the pose. Where an arm is held limp, let your lines also be limp. Where a foot is pushing off the floor, let your lines also push off the floor.

Try not to draw the appearance of the model. Rather, try to draw the activity of the model. Your hand and your lines should do what the model is doing. Don't fixate on one visual attribute, contour for example. Rush rapidly from part to part, never lingering anywhere too long. Be in a hurry to establish the whole pose.

Later on, alternate poses by the model, and slide views of buildings and bridges. Do gesture drawings of both. As you draw, try to transfer the ease with which you draw from the figure to your drawing from buildings.[18]

---

[18] Adapted from "Gesture," in Kimon Nicholaides, *The Natural Way to Draw*, pp. 14–20.

Figure 1.65 Jean Gieger and Albert Kim.

Figure 1.66 Rebecca Schultz.

Comments: *In practice, one of the most important applications of gesture drawing is in making quick diagrammatic plans of buildings. As in this plan view by Louis I. Kahn of the Morris house, the shared intention between the two, the plan and the figure drawing, lies in the fact that both are directed at expressing essential properties in a few quick lines.*

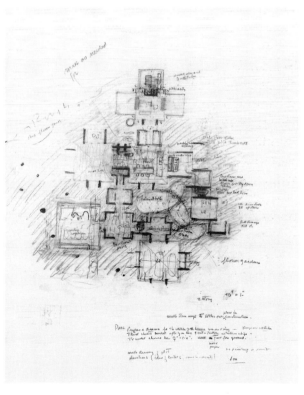

Figure 1.67 Louis I. Kahn. Plan for Morris House. Louis I. Kahn Collection, University of Pennsylvania and the Pennsylvania Historical and Museum Commission.

SPACES AND VOIDS

Perceiving Solids and Voids

We have a fairly clear sense of how we perceive solids. Solids are the material part, the "stuff" of the environment. They are the parts we bump into. They are the things the radar bounces off. But what about the other part, the empty space? How do we perceive that? This is not an easy question to answer because empty space generates no sensation. It's empty.

I once lived in Siena, Italy, for several months, a city where the buildings are closely packed and the streets quite narrow—so narrow in fact that I remember many times having to quickly back up flat against the buildings facing the street whenever a bus passed by. Most of the streets are not straight; they are laid out to conform to the shape of the land. They follow level contours or the spines of Siena's multiple ridges and valleys. Nevertheless, though it didn't follow the familiar American grid pattern, the environment seemed very readable. Most puzzling of all, the empty spaces in the town, the streets and piazzas, seemed to have discernible shapes of their own. How did they?

One thing we can say immediately about space in Siena is that there's less of it. Owing to the close packing of the houses, empty space is a much rarer commodity than in a typical American environment, such as a suburban housing development or strip mall. In the United States empty space abounds. Most buildings are object-buildings made of relatively thin members such as wood, steel, and precast concrete. They tend to be freestanding on individual plots, with lots of space between.

Looking at the plan of Siena and noticing how densely packed it is, we might state as a law of sorts that *where space is rare it tends to be more readable as space.* An 8-foot-wide bus racing toward us on a 14-foot-wide street in Siena provides us with a spatial experience that is vivid indeed. The same bus on an American boulevard driving past a strip mall is scarcely cause for alarm. For similar reasons (rarity of space versus prevalence of space) a mariner sailing through a narrow passage such as the Strait of Magellan proceeds with much greater caution than on the open ocean. In such situations, the dimensions of space are understood, even felt, because they simply must be attended to.

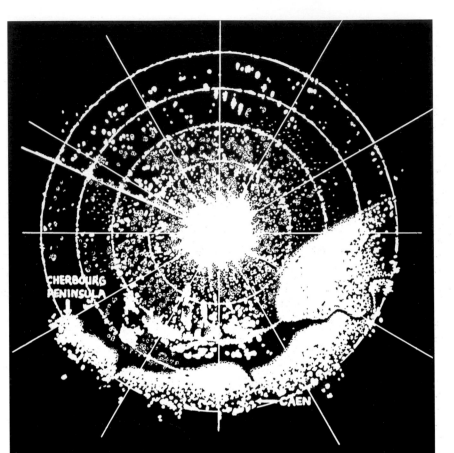

Figure 1.68 Radar view of the Normandy beaches on D-Day. We cannot sense empty space; only the solids provide sensation. Solids are the part the radar bounces off.

Space as Figure

Nature is replete with circumstances where space is rarer and the solid more prevalent. Like the strait mentioned above, harbors, bays, sounds, channels, and seas are all conditions where a body of water is shaped by the surrounding and more prevalent dry land.

Figure 1.69 Plan of Siena. Where space is rarer, it is also more compelling as a figural element.

Muschelplatz (the clam-shaped piazza). Americans compare it to a fan. It is interesting that both of these words refer to solids. And this fact is precisely the point. Where the shape of a space is so distinct that it may be compared to a solid, empty space takes on a peculiar quality. Though it cannot be sensed as a thing, it is nevertheless understood as a thing in its own right. In what we may characterize as a true figure-ground reversal, we come to understand space as the inverse of a solid.

The exercises that follow are directed at developing our ability to understand space as a figural element. To accomplish this, we will put ourselves in unfamiliar territory. As in the sectional drawing in Figure 1.70, we will draw the space instead of the solid.

Figure 1.70 Rick Marron. We will draw the space instead of the solid.

Even more compelling, empty space takes on a particularly powerful read when we are also able to perceive it as the missing part of a solid. One reason the Grand Canyon inspires such awe is that we are still aware of the flat plateau that was once there.

But while consideration of the relative rarity of space and space as the missing part of a solid may help us understand the streets in Siena, what of the piazzas? They are at times vast. The central piazza, the Campo, measures some 500 feet across. But readable it is, so readable in fact that people often name it with comparative words. Germans call it *Der*

Figure 1.71 Bill Birkholz.

Figure 1.72 Patricia Clark.

Figure 1.73 Teri Tsang.

SPACE 1

Paint the spaces between.

Ink, ¼" brush, bond paper

Construct a still life that has interesting spaces between the solids. Bicycles, ladders, and crates are good subjects. Then, with brushed ink, draw these spaces.

As you draw, try to understand volume as the figural element of the composition. Though it is somewhat more difficult, avoid generating the spaces by drawing their outlines first. Generate them outward from their centers.

Comments: It is helpful to think of the action of your brush as analogous to the stick of a blind man probing a space. First he finds the empty space, then he moves the stick around the space until he taps its edges. Your brush should move in this way: first center the space, then find its edges.

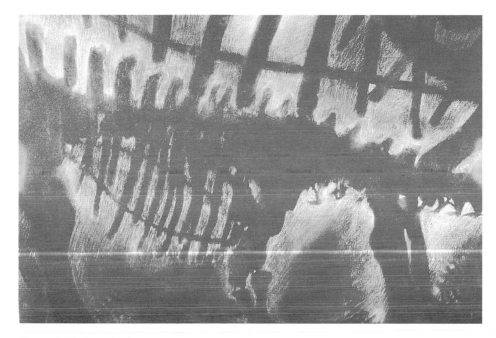

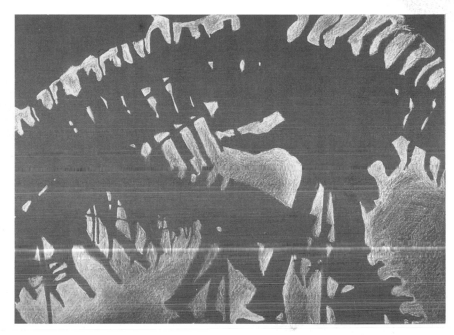

Figure 1.74 Brent Buck.

Figure 1.75 Nell Babra.

SPACE 2

Draw the spaces between.

White prismacolor, black construction paper

View a skeleton from a direction that has interesting and articulate spaces among the bones. Compose your view in a way that supports understanding volume as the figural element in the drawing. For example, avoid centering the skeleton on the page. That would emphasize your sense of it as an object.

Then, with white colored-pencil, draw the spaces between the bones. Where the bones

are, leave the paper blank. While you draw, pay attention to the marks on the paper. Try to make them contribute to a figural reading of space. Though it's more difficult, do not generate the voids by drawing their outlines first. Build them outward from their centers.

Comments: *One of the more interesting intentions to pursue in this exercise is to give the drawing a sense of multiple depths, despite its limitation to only two variables — space or solid. The two examples in Figures 1.74 and 1.75 have taken two very different approaches. The one at the left shows two skeletons at different distances and uses the relative sizes of the spaces between the bones and the skeleton themselves to establish depth.[19] The other, in an approach implying atmospheric perspective, defines the edges of nearer spaces more precisely than the edges of further spaces.[20]*

---

[19] This is called size perspective. A sense of depth arises from the relative projected sizes of objects at various distances from the observer. See also p. 90.

[20] Atmospheric perspective: The air has an effect on the visual acuity of objects at various distances from the observer. Closer objects seem clearer. Further objects seem fuzzier. See also p. 92.

SPACE 3

Give the spaces depth.

Conté crayon, newsprint

Now we can begin to give depth to the spaces in between. We will make distinctions between their deeper and shallower areas.

Walk into a deep forest or go to a plant conservatory. Find an array of foliage that has well-articulated depth and interesting spaces between the leaves. The scene will likely have distinct layers of foliage that document several positions of depth.

With conté crayon or soft charcoal, describe the spaces in between as deeper and shallower. Where the volume between you and the foliage is deeper, your drawing should become darker; where the volume between you and the foliage is shallower, your drawing should remain lighter. In the end, you should seek to achieve a murky and highly atmospheric sense of depth, not unlike that of an extremely foggy day.

Figure 1.76 Andrew Kikta.

Comments: *There are two distinct ways to start this exercise that come immediately to mind: 1) start with the spaces furthest away; 2) start with the closest spaces. I find it better to start with the space that seems the most prominent in giving the scene shape. This space may be closer or further (more likely it's in the middle-ground), but its most important attribute is that it organizes and gives location to the scene's many subparts.*

For the sense of feeling the space as you draw, it is important to work from the general to the specific. The small drawing in Figure 1.80 is only partly complete, and its history, from its earliest marks to its most complete state, is still evident. Note the area at the left. This is how you should work — vaguely, noncommittally, tentatively, at the start, always ready to modify shape and value as needed.

Figure 1.77 Esther I. Chen.

Figure 1.78 Eric Newhouse.

Figure 1.79 Tanvir N. Bashar.

Figure 1.80 Lyanne Schuster.

SPACE 4

Make the volume between.

Charcoal (soft black), newsprint

Find a broad building façade that has a variety of openings. Pick a diagonal view.

Then, with charcoal, describe the depth of the volume between you and the façade. Where the volume between you and the façade is deep, draw darker; where the volume between you and the façade is shallow, draw lighter.

Comments: *As you draw, try to believe that you are making the atmosphere that fills the distance between you and the façade. Just as in the previous exercise, your drawing should give the volume a material character. It should seem murky and soupy, like a foggy day.*

Figure 1.81 Rebecca Schultz.

Figure 1.82 Anthony Wee.

Figure 1.83 Tanvir N. Bashar.

SPACE 5

Make the volume within.

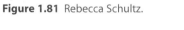

Pick an architectural subject that has a dominant internal space. A good subject might be a grouping of columns, such as the pulpit shown in Figure 1.81, the space beneath a heavy and ornate table, or a large hall with multiple structural bays. If you can't find a suitable architectural subject, a skeleton or an arrangement of bicycles would do.

Then, with charcoal, describe the thickness of the space within the subject. In the sense that you strive to give the space a material quality, you should draw as you did in the previous exercise, make the volume between, but in this instance, consciously try to occupy the internal space with your charcoal while you draw.

Comments: *I find that a mark angling from upper right to lower left as in Figure 1.81 (or from upper left to lower right, if you are left-handed) is particularly effective in giving a sense of atmosphere to the space.*

Figure 1.84 Joseph Romano.

SPACE 6

Draw the space within a section.

Pencil, illustration board

This exercise and the two that follow aim to build a more spatial understanding of plans, sections, and elevations, the conventional drawings that architects and designers use. In them we use the same atmospheric sense of space we have been using in the preceding exercises.

In a sectional view, describe the depth of the space within a building with charcoal tone. Where the space is deeper, draw darker. Where the space is shallower, draw lighter. Try to bring to this exercise two characteristics from your earlier work: a sense of the depth between you and the distant surfaces of the building and a sense that you are occupying the space with your charcoal as you draw.

It is important to pick an appropriate building for this exercise. It should have a dominant central space and recognizable overlapping elements in the background such as arcades and stairways.

In the spirit of the highly rendered drawings of the Beaux Arts, this exercise also lends itself to watercolor.

Comments: *Once again, note how the linework contributes to the drawing's atmospheric feeling.*

SPACE 7

Draw the depth in an elevation.

Ebony pencil, white prismacolor, chipboard

This exercise, which I conduct as a group exercise, has the same objective as the previous one, though it represents depth somewhat differently. In the previous exercise, you darkened only those areas that were further away. In effect, you considered the white page as a foreground of sorts. The surface for this exercise is neutral gray, and you use it as a middle-ground. From that middle-ground you operate in two directions, both forward and back. You use ebony pencil to depress certain areas and you use white prismacolor to pull other areas forward.

Begin by just laying out all the chipboard pieces on the floor and roughing in the location of major elements. Choreograph the process so that groups of students work in sub-groups and then muster back together to consider the drawing as a whole once more. There is much to be gained from this experience. It closely parallels the thought process of an individual working alone—working the parts back to the whole—but it does so in a way that physically acts out the cognitive process. The panels and the participants disperse, and then they come back together again.

Doing it as a group (I have used groups as large as 50) brings another important side benefit: the students teach each other. Simply through the adjacency of stronger students to weaker students, stronger and more focused thinking guides the work of the weaker students as they try to maintain a seamless appearance across the whole drawing. This exercise is a case of the whole being greater than the sum of its parts. It is an enormous confidence builder for the weaker students, who would never imagine they could contribute to a process that results in such an impressive work!

Comments: *I have to raise an important note of caution here with respect to this and the previous exercises on space. Although this kind of volumetric drawing does* not *address the issue of illumination — it's about giving a material property to depth — because of its rendered appearance, it often gives the impression that it does. Students may therefore mistakenly conclude that, as a convention of drawing, it is always better to darken areas that are further from the viewer. As it concerns illumination, sometimes it is indeed the case that areas that are further are darker. But they also sometimes appear lighter or neutral.*

Figure 1.85 Façade of S. Gilles. First-Year Group Project co-taught with Jill Watson. Class included: Hajime Ando, Nick Arauz, Lisa Aufman, Ben Bell, Colin Brice, Scott Chiang, Michael Gallin, Nicholas Hague, Kenneth Kim, Judy Lee, Peter McLaughlin, Alan Mizuki, Richard Monopoli, Michael O' Sullivan, Michael Parris, Basil Richardson, Sean Starkweather, Zaidi Tuah.

Figure 1.86 *Ceramics Cooperative.* Patrick Sutton.

SPACE 8

A design project focusing on volume.

Charcoal on vellum

From time to time, I have taught architectural design projects that have used the same volumetric representations as the previous exercises. Like those exercises, these projects treated volume as the figural element of the composition from the start. They fostered understanding of plans, sections, and elevations that went beyond an understanding of a building's material; they addressed the building's space as well. In all of the projects, it was assumed that the buildings were to be carved out or eroded out of a preexisting monolith.

I want to highlight several important characteristics of these projects:

Space is rare. With the beginning condition of a monolith occupying the entire potential volume of the site, at the outset, solid material is maximized. It is everywhere. More importantly, empty space is minimized. It is nowhere to be found. This is the exact opposite of the beginning condition of most design problems. As a consequence, volumes are generated from the direction of their minimal possible sizes, rather than, as is normal, from their maximum. In this way, it is easier to address the important question of the minimal volumes required for the activities within an architectural program.

Volume is figure. Since form is generated by making volume, rather than by making material, volume naturally becomes the more obvious figure of the design. Drawing is analogous to the act of building. In the manner of the previous exercises, pressing harder into the paper is mechanically parallel to depressing surfaces in the building.

The project. The project shown in Figure 1.86 used a ceramics cooperative for its program. It assumed a limestone monolith 30' high × 120' wide × 160' deep in a warehouse district in Los Angeles.

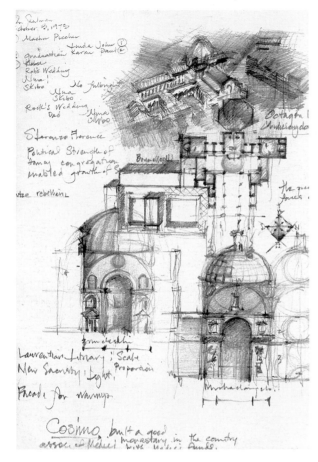

Figure 1.87 Notes from a class. Andrew Tesoro, 1975.

Figure 1.88 Plan and section of the Pantheon. Andrew Tesoro, 1977.

SPACE IN PRACTICE

My good friend, New York architect Andrew Tesoro, has long made use of drawings that show space as a figural element of design. Drawings he completed as notes in an architecture history lecture course show this early fascination (Figure 1.87). Later travel sketches, such as that of the superimposed plan and section of the Pantheon (Figure 1.88) carried this understanding further. As a practitioner today, he often makes drawings such as the one shown in Figure 1.89 to present to himself the "shape of space," even as he accounts in other drawings for the material facts of what he is proposing.

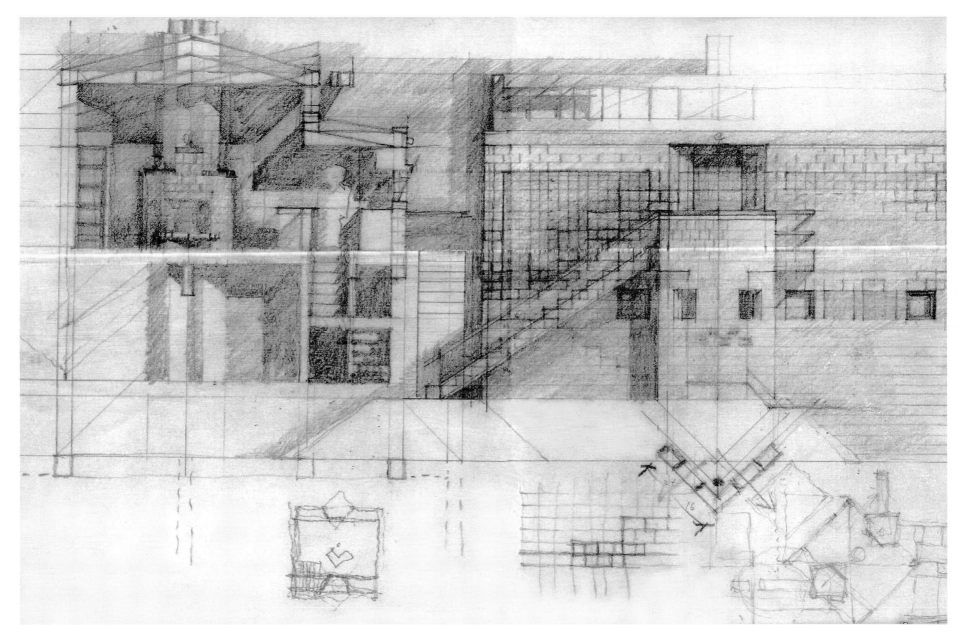

Figure 1.89 Study for Galeza House, Andrew Tesoro, 1985.

The Order of Appearance

A foundation based on the teaching
of James J. Gibson

GIBSON AND TEXTURAL GRADIENT

The Ecological Understanding

With the kinesthetic foundation of Kimon Nicholaides' exercises in the first chapter firmly established, we can now move to a more analytical approach to the question of appearance. Views on the issue are numerous, but this chapter focuses on one: the early work of the perceptual psychologist James J. Gibson, as presented in his landmark first book, *The Perception of the Visual World*.[1]

Gibson, the leader of the so-called ecological view of perception, began his work during the early stages of World War II. He was contracted by the United States government to help in the development of what amounted to a forerunner of present-day flight simulators. Early in the war, many pilot trainees were crashing on their first flights. To better prepare them before putting them in the air, Gibson needed to gain a better understanding of the visual environment of flight.

Though he would modify it considerably later on,[2] out of this early work on flight, Gibson proposed a fundamentally new position with respect to visual perception. While not entirely discounting the roles of predisposition or perceptual learning,[3] Gibson argued that perception is based primarily on the structure of the environment. With respect to vision, he concluded that light enters our eyes in a state that is already ordered by the planes and surfaces from which it has been reflected. For Gibson, the sensory data of the world already possesses sufficient order such that perceiving can proceed on it alone.

This is an important point of view for architects and designers, and its importance goes beyond the fact that Gibson clarifies phenomena that are complicated and in dispute. Architects and designers must design for the general public; they must presume the possibility of a spatial order that works for all. The central tenant of the ecological point of view, that sensation is in itself already ordered, is an absolutist argument. Its limitations not withstanding, it is valuable precisely because it is free from relativist individual and cultural concerns. As he proposes it, Gibson's order is universal, applicable for every time, for everyone, everywhere. What is the nature of the order that Gibson found to be so universal in the visual environment?

Gibson found that order in the visual textures of the material world. Beginning with his wartime investigations of pilot disorientation during "whiteouts," Gibson came to believe that illumination is *not* the key issue for vi-

Figure 2.1 For Gibson, the world is already ordered as it enters our eyes.

sion. Perception of surface and surface texture is. And Gibson came to believe that we perceive surface through the visual textures of which materials are made.

Visual Texture and Textural Gradient

For Gibson, "visual texture" is a broadly inclusive term. In *The Perception of the Visual World*, he includes textures that are artificial as well

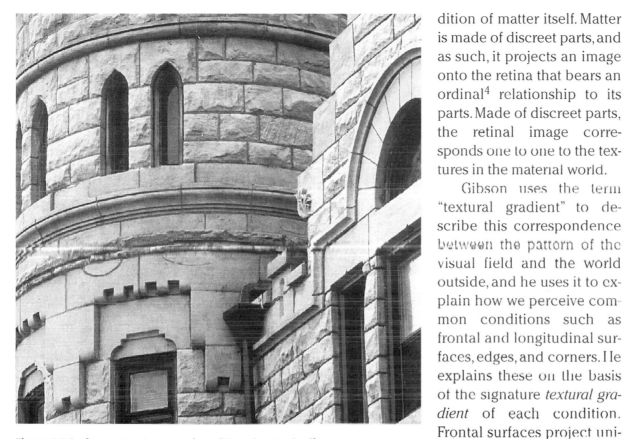

Figure 2.2 Surface texture is a natural condition of matter itself.

as natural, whether a floor of square tiles or a lawn of blades of grass. He includes textures at multiple scales, considering both the cornstalks of an individual field and the patchwork of farms that make up a midwest landscape. He includes textures of all sorts of shapes and compositions, whether rectangular bricks in walls or round telephone poles in rows. Gibson finds texture to be a natural condition of matter itself. Matter is made of discreet parts, and as such, it projects an image onto the retina that bears an ordinal[4] relationship to its parts. Made of discreet parts, the retinal image corresponds one to one to the textures in the material world.

Gibson uses the term "textural gradient" to describe this correspondence between the pattern of the visual field and the world outside, and he uses it to explain how we perceive common conditions such as frontal and longitudinal surfaces, edges, and corners. He explains these on the basis of the signature *textural gradient* of each condition. Frontal surfaces project uniform gradients. Longitudinal surfaces, such as floors and streets, project gradients that diminish with greater distance from the observer. Corners and edges project gradients that shift abruptly from the gradient in one orientation or distance to the gradient in another.

Gradients, Depth Cues, and the Exercises

The next pages present and illustrate the perception of various signature conditions in the visual world. These are followed by a series of exercises. The first explore the issue of texture, material, and depth in a manner that is independent of linear perspective—in effect, where Gibson began. The later exercises serve as a transition to introduce perspective.

[1] James J. Gibson, *The Perception of the Visual World* (Boston: Houghton Mifflin Co., 1950), Chapters 1–9.

[2] Gibson developed and modified this view in two subsequent books. In the first, *The Senses Considered as Perceptual Systems* (Boston: Houghton Mifflin, 1966), he gave greater emphasis to the contribution of both kinesthetic interaction with the environment and the interaction of the senses with each other. In the second, *The Ecological Approach to Visual Perception* (Boston: Houghton Mifflin, 1979), he emphasized motion parallax as the key characteristic of the optical array.

[3] Gestalt psychology emphasizes the role of predisposing laws governing the perception of form. Transactional psychology emphasizes the role of perceptual learning or interaction with the environment as the basis for perception.

[4] The order of the intervals in the retinal image matches the order of the projected surface.

PERCEIVING A FLAT FRONTAL SURFACE

Figure 2.3 Liberty Center, Urban Design Associates, Pittsburgh, Pennsylvania.

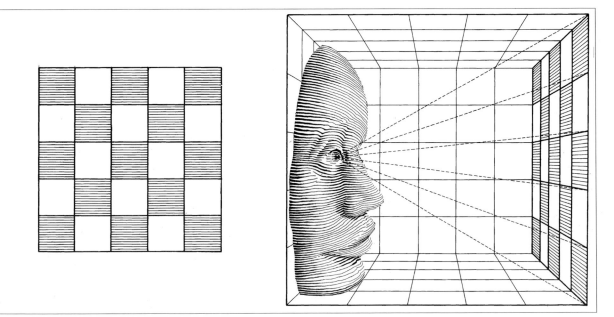

PERCEIVING A FLAT FRONTAL SURFACE

Figure 2.4 A flat frontal surface projects an array of stimuli onto the retina whose gradient (interval between stimuli) is constant.

PERCEIVING A FLAT LONGITUDINAL SURFACE
Figure 2.5 Street paving. (Photo: Raymond Mall).

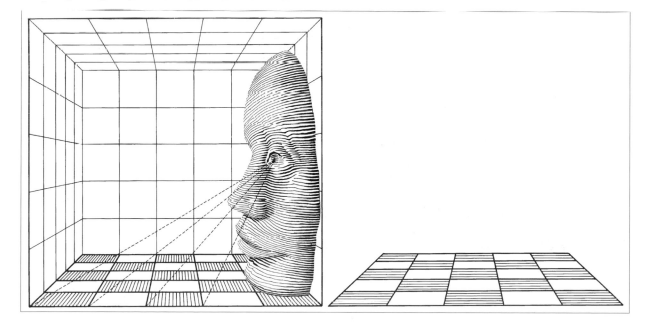

PERCEIVING A FLAT LONGITUDINAL SURFACE
Figure 2.6 A flat longitudinal surface projects an array of stimuli onto the retina, whose gradient decreases and nears the center of the retina with increasing distance from the observer.

PERCEIVING A FLAT SLANTING SURFACE
Figure 2.7 Awnings and roofs above Kennywood Park.

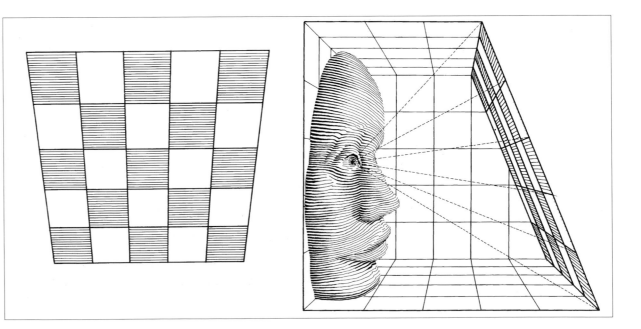

PERCEIVING A FLAT SLANTING SURFACE
Figure 2.8 A flat slanting surface projects an array of stimuli onto the retina, whose gradient decreases and nears the center of the retina either more or less rapidly than that of a longitudinal surface.

PERCEIVING A ROUNDED SURFACE
Figure 2.9 Three Rivers Stadium.

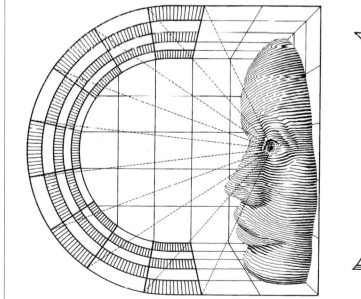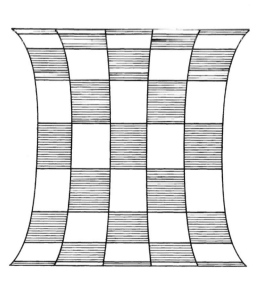

PERCEIVING A ROUNDED SURFACE
Figure 2.10 A rounded surface projects an array of stimuli onto the retina, whose gradient changes from small to large to small as the surface curves from a longitudinal to a frontal and back to a longitudinal attitude relative to the observer.

PERCEIVING A CORNER
Figure 2.11 Liberty Center, Urban Design Associates, Pittsburgh, Pennsylvania.

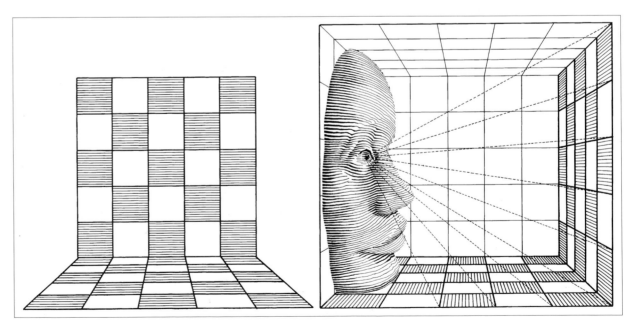

PERCEIVING A CORNER
Figure 2.12 A corner of a surface projects an array of stimuli onto the retina, whose gradient abruptly shifts from one corresponding to that surface in one attitude to one corresponding to that surface in another attitude.

Figure 2.13 Post Office, Federal Building, and Gulf Building.

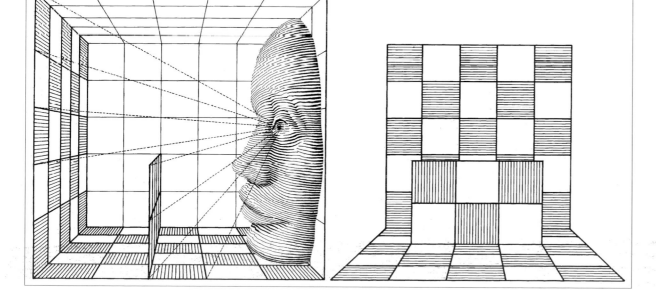

Figure 2.14 An edge of a surface projects an array of stimuli onto the retina, whose gradient abruptly shifts from one corresponding to that surface to one corresponding to the surface of a background.

TEXTURAL GRADIENT AND FORM 1
Deformed surface pattern.[5]

Pencil, bond paper, printed cloth or woven material

According to Gibson, the presence of adequate illumination is insufficient as a basis for perception. The presence of surface texture is the key. This exercise is directed at the role of pattern and repetition in our perception of surface.

Select an article of clothing or a drape that has a repeating pattern woven into or printed onto its surface. Stripes, checkerboards, or even plaids are appropriate. Arrange the cloth so that a series of interesting folds is created and so that you can infer the form of the cloth solely as a function of the deformation of the regular pattern caused by these folds.

Draw the pattern. Draw only the pattern. Do not draw the outlines of the cloth or the folds, except as they may be parts of the deformation of the pattern itself. Do not describe the variation of light on the surface.

[5]Assignment from Professor Randall Korman, Syracuse University.

Figure 2.15 David McKee.

TEXTURAL GRADIENT AND FORM 2
Profile, materiality, and surface texture.

Carbon pencil, charcoal paper

Surface texture is a natural condition of material. Materials have discrete parts, and according to Gibson, these discrete parts are the basis of our perception. Among things as diverse as pineapples, with their diamond pattern, and limestone cliffs, with their layers of sedimentary rock, we understand surface form as a variant of formation textures. Likewise, we perceive edges and profiles as abrupt shifts of textural gradients from one corresponding to a foreground material to one corresponding to a background material. This exercise builds understanding of the contributions of texture to both form and profile.

Select at least three interesting objects that have obvious repeating material textures. Pineapples, reed baskets, and shredded-wheat biscuits are examples of good choices. Arrange the objects in an interesting way so that they overlap each other from your point of view.

Draw the still life as an array of various surface textures. Pay careful attention to the characteristic textures of the individual materials as well as to the ways in which these textures deform with variations of shape.

Figure 2.16 David McKee.

TEXTURAL GRADIENT AND FORM 3
Surface and distance of view.[6]

Charcoal, newsprint

So far, we have drawn material textures at a size where we could feel fairly confident that what we were drawing was the actual material of the object. But many material textures are subsensory. Consider for a moment the texture of skin. We have only to look for a moment at a close-up photograph of skin, an image that might show canyonlike fissures and frightening bacteria, to realize how many of its material properties we have (perhaps thankfully) failed to register.

With such materials we often have to invent textures to represent them. While these textures must share certain formal properties with the original, they do not necessarily represent textures that are physically present on the original. The engraver of a dollar bill does not, after all, actually believe that Washington's face was covered with horizontal stripes. Rather, these stripes indicate how Washington's face would appear if it were made of stripes, and on this conditional basis we are still able to perceive his face.

This exercise poses a similar problem of inventing surface texture, but in this case it

---

[6] Assignment adapted from an assignment from Professor Delbert Highlands, Carnegie Mellon University.

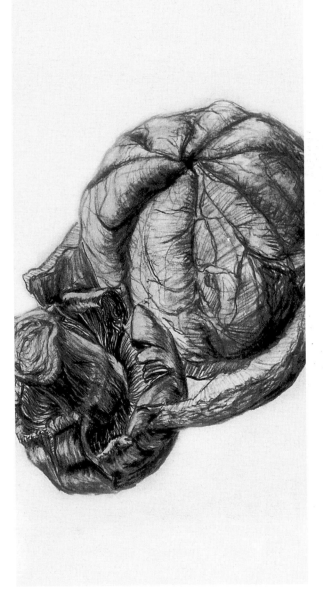
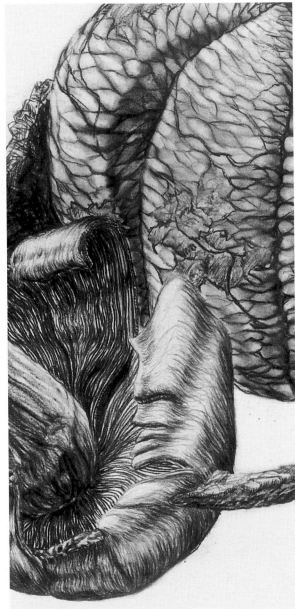

Figures 2.17, 2.18, 2.19, 2.20 Paul Shea.

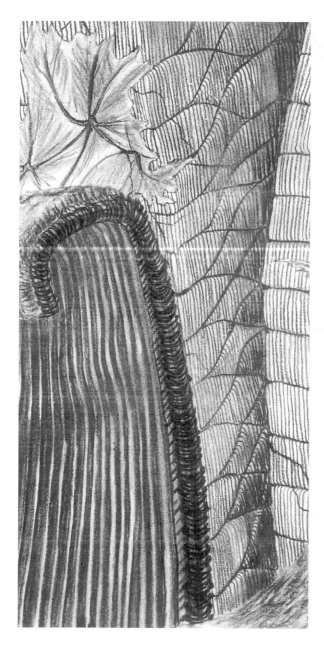

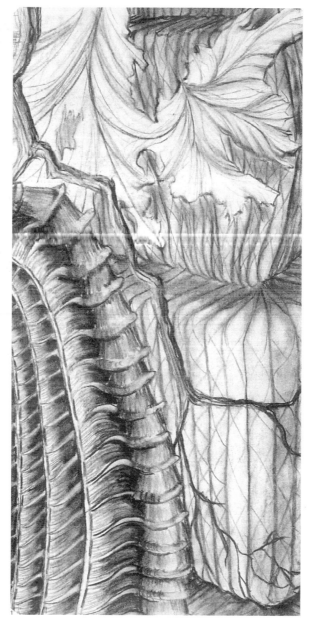

operates by enlarging the size of what is shown. In drawing the nearer views of this assignment, you will be put in the position of having to invent the textures you are drawing.

Select two kinds of food of contrasting surface texture, such as meat and bread or butter and crackers. Arrange them so that one object overlaps the other. Then draw a series of views describing an approach toward a point along the overlapping edge. Keep drawing views until you achieve a view in which the identity of the original foods is no longer discernible.[7]

[7] As an extension of this exercise, try the following: After having reached the point at which the identities of the materials are lost, redefine the two materials. Then draw a series of views describing a withdrawal from the overlapping edge between these two new materials. In effect, you will have transformed the original materials into two new materials through a process of analysis, a process of breaking a material into its constituent parts.

TEXTURAL GRADIENT AND FORM 4
Organic form.

Charcoal, newsprint

This project aims at uniting the earlier studies in this chapter on material textures with some initial indications of variation of light on surfaces. The primary medium will be charcoal, and the study will include a range of both fragmentary sketches and completed drawings.

The project begins with the theme of forms that grow lengthwise. Subjects include animal horns, hooves, and teeth, as well as branches of trees. Later themes will be material, surface, and light. Subjects for these studies will be wood, fur, skin, feathers, scales, and the like. The overall aim of this project is to gain knowledge of various materials and shapes, as they are perceived in various conditions of light.

Figure 2.21 Jeffrey Pitchford.

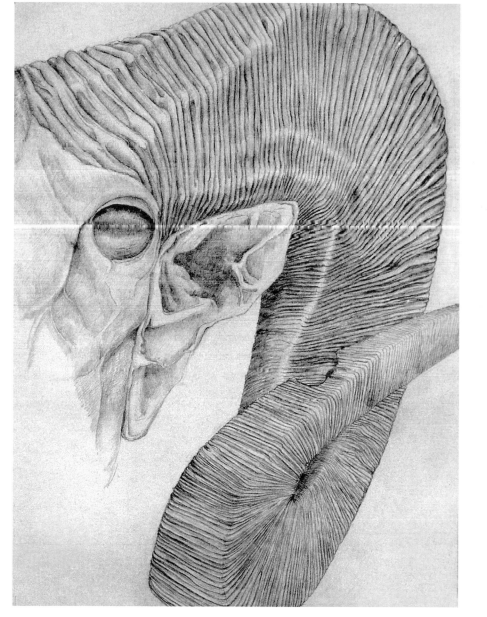

Figure 2.22 David McKee.

Figure 2.23 Scot Wallace.

Figure 2.24 Paula McLay Maynes.

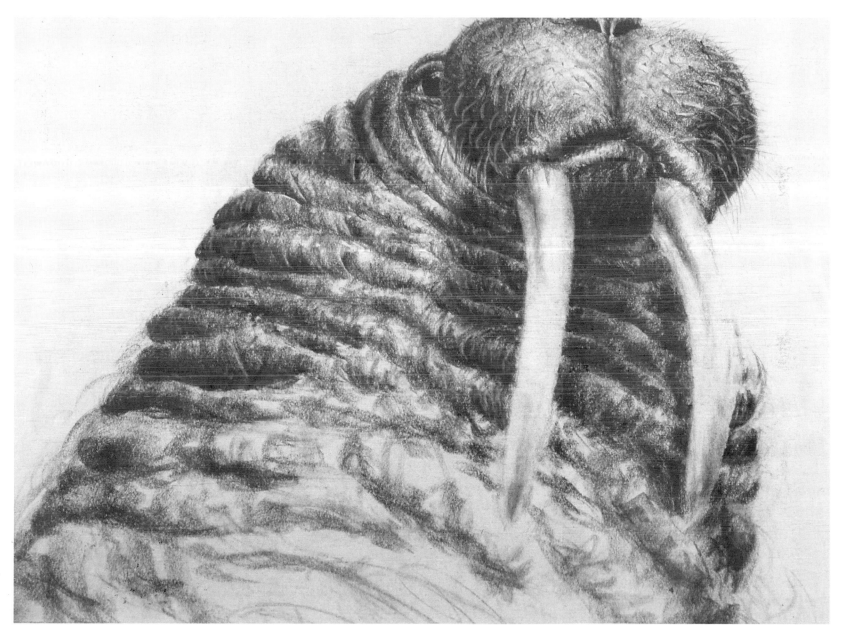

Figure 2.25 Holly Wasilowski.

Figure 2.26 John C. Ferri.

Figure 2.27 Will Bossert.

Figure 2.28 Will Bossert.

TEXTURAL GRADIENT AND FORM 5

When texture implies perspective.

Conté, newsprint

You have grown skilled by now at recognizing how the material properties of things carry information about their formal properties. But what of the artificial world? And what of environments where objects are more architectural in character?

This is a transitional exercise, intended to sharpen our understanding of visual texture so that we can build our understanding of linear perspective upon it. Find a building with an interesting array of decorative elements. Shaped cornices, ornately carved frames around windows and doorways, terra cotta friezes, and soffits are the kinds of details to look for.

Focusing on their decorative textures, draw some of these details from an angular direction. The angle at which you draw the object is key. Pick an angle such that parallel edges on your subject seem to converge. Avoid frontal directions of view that might allow these edges to remain nearly parallel.

Figure 2.29 Patricia Clark.

Figure 2.30 Vincent Chew.

TEXTURAL GRADIENT AND FORM 6

From texture to perspective.

Conté, newsprint

Like the previous one, this exercise is aimed at building our understanding of linear perspective upon Gibson's understanding of the textural gradient. We intend to treat perspective as merely a special case of the textural gradi-

ent, one in which, owing to their formation, material textures tend to recede to common vanishing points. In short, we aim to derive perspective as a material fact of the visual field, much as Gibson has defined it for us.

For your subject, look for repeated elements and intervals at multiple scales: at a smaller scale, bricks, boards, and the like; at a larger scale, window and column intervals.

Focusing on these elements, and considering their role in the larger order of the building, draw a large portion of the building as a textural array. Again, pay close attention to the direction of your view. Fairly steep angles are usually better. And in this exercise, in contrast to the previous one, you need to stand far enough back to sense the perspective of the whole scene.

GIBSON AND DEPTH CUES

Cues Based on the Environment

After presenting the role textural gradient plays in our perception of surfaces, corners, and profiles (the building blocks of the visual field, so to speak), Gibson goes on to discuss *depth cues*. Depth cues are conditions of the visual field— one object overlapping another, for example— that commonly yield perceptions of depth. Though others had identified them before, Gibson contributed greatly to our understanding of their nature. What stands out in his explanation is the way it proceeds from his discussion of textural gradient. As in that discussion, the characteristic conditions in the environment and their signature array of textural gradients remain central in his explanations of depth cues.

As his predecessors had done, Gibson breaks the list of depth cues into two groups: primary cues and secondary cues. The first group, numbering three cues, is dependent upon either the existence of two eyes or upon subtle sensations of muscular response. These cues are effective within only short distances from the observer; and because they are less involved with the conditions of the environment, for the purposes of Gibson's central argument (which is an argument about the environment), these cues are less important.

Figure 2.31 For Gibson, textural gradient is a natural condition of the environment (Photo: Larry Rumbaugh).

Primary Cues

The three primary cues are:

1. *Accommodation.* Based on the changing focal length required in focusing objects at various distances from the observer.
2. *Disparity vision.* Based on the disparity of the views between the two eyes.
3. *Convergence.* Based on the angle at which the eyes must converge in focusing on objects at various distances from the observer.

Secondary Cues

The second group of seven cues, by far the more interesting to Gibson, had been treated as less important by those preceding Gibson. Indeed, one of Gibson's great contributions was in upgrading the importance of these cues. Gibson's predecessors had treated them as a set of special cases that are partly learned, whereas Gibson explains them with the textural gradient, something that is not learned. Though he, too, considers them to be special

This flower appears smaller and nearer to the horizon; therefore it is farther

This flower appears larger and further from the horizon; therefore It Is closer

Figure 2.32 He bases his understanding of depth cues on textural gradient (Photo: Larry Rumbaugh).

cases, for him they are special cases of the information from the environment, the continuous surface texture of the world around us. Thus, he considers linear perspective as a special case arising when surfaces in the environmental have parallel alignments, and size perspective as a special case of the density of textures at various distances. For Gibson, these cues arise as a natural correspondence between the retinal image and an environment made of discrete parts.

The secondary cues are the more interesting for our purposes as well because, except for motion parallax, they can all be replicated by drawing. They might even be called the *pictorial cues*. I list them here in the order in which, in my observation, they are acquired as conventions for use in making drawings. This brief listing is followed with more lengthy explanations of each cue, which address two issues: the information signature of the cue and its use as a convention in drawing. The secondary cues are:

1. *Distance from the horizon line.* Based on the tendency of objects to appear nearer the horizon line with greater distance from the observer.
2. *Overlap.* Based on the tendency of near objects to overlap far objects.
3. *Shade and shadow.* Based on three-dimensional modeling of objects in light, shade, and shadow.
4. *Size perspective.* Based on the apparent reduction in size of objects with greater distance from the observer.
5. *Atmospheric perspective.* Based on the effect of the atmosphere on the color and visual acuity of objects at various distances from the observer.
6. *Linear perspective.* Based on the apparent convergence of parallel lines to common vanishing points with increasing distance from the observer.
7. *Motion parallax.* Based on apparent relative motions of objects at various distances from the observer when the observer is moving.

DISTANCE FROM THE HORIZON LINE

Objects approach the horizon line with greater distance from the viewer.

Its Signature

It is a fact of optics that objects seen in the foreground tend to overlap their backgrounds. The tops of trees overlap the background sky; columns overlap the ceiling they support; tables overlap the floor on which they rest. The positions at which objects appear to meet background surfaces indicate their distance from an observer. The base of a nearer column will appear *lower* against its background floor and further from the horizon line (the height of the observer's eyes in the view). Conversely, the base of a more distant column will appear *higher* against the same floor, and thus nearer to the horizon line.

Its Use in Drawing, a Special Case: Upward Position in the Visual Field

Two characteristics of our environment tend to make this cue apply more readily to conditions below the horizon line than above. First, we live on the Earth's surface, a condition dominated by gravity. Most things we see in daily life tend to be located near the ground, and logically we tend to think of their locations in terms of that ground surface. Second, we are upright beings, and so much of the time view the world from a relatively elevated standing position. From this point of view, most objects of interest appear arrayed against a back-

Figure 2.33 Distance from the horizon line indicates distance from an observer.

ground below the horizon line, much as tables and chairs appear located against the background of the floor on which they rest.

Thus when we make drawings, we can easily represent basic positional relationships merely by locating things higher on the ground if they are farther or lower if they are nearer. This practice of positioning things higher in the visual field to indicate greater depth is used by many cultures, even those that historically have not used linear perspective. In addition to *atmospheric perspective*, it is the central pictorial convention of Chinese and Japanese landscapes.

Perhaps because of its simplicity, this convention, which we will call *upward position in the visual field*, tends to be the first depth cue used by children. Children as young as 5 com-

Figure 2.34 The road is nearer. The house is further. The mountains are furthest.

gerated the amount of visible floor surface in the view, a tendency that commonly plagues novices in perspective drawing.

> Doug: "I think you're showing more floor surface than should be apparent."
>
> Student: "But it's a deep space, and I wanted to make it look deep."

Almost as a case of life imitating art, the observation is thrown off by the earlier use of upward position in the visual field. Greater depth seems to translate almost automatically into higher in the visual field.

Observations of overhead surfaces, surfaces above the horizon line such as ceilings, beams, and roof overhangs, are made particularly difficult by misunderstanding the convention of upward position. Above the horizon line, conditions reverse. Look at the view in Figure 2.33. The nearer column touches the beam higher in the visual field. The farther column touches it lower in the field.

Distance from the Horizon Line: A Better Way to Understand the Cue

Because of this confusion, the only unified way to understand how depth can be inferred from the position of objects on their backgrounds is to understand the cue in its relationship to the horizon line. Whether above or below the viewer's height, those things appearing closer to the horizon line are further from the observer; those things further from the horizon line are nearer to the observer.

monly use it, and all of us at between ages 5 and 7 have probably made drawings very much like the one in Figure 2.34, with the road in the foreground, the house in the middle-ground, and the mountain in the distance—all laid out such that higher in the picture indicates further.

But this convention is not without its problems. Though optically related to linear perspective, later in life upward position in the visual field seems to distort some observations, which are necessary for mature perspective drawing. It is as if some vestige of this earlier convention makes linear perspective more difficult to acquire.

I have often had exchanges along the following lines when I have sat down to comment on a student's perspective that has exag-

OVERLAP (AND MOTION PARALLAX)

Based on the tendency of near objects to overlap far objects.

Its Signature

According to Gibson, readings of overlapping edges arise in abrupt shifts of textural gradient, from the gradient of the material in front to that of the material behind. Of the pictorial cues, *overlap* seems the most definitive. Though by no means foolproof,[8] an apparent overlap seems to establish exactly what is in front of what.

I would speculate that the reason overlaps seem so compelling owes to their relationship to *motion parallax*.[9] When we move, nearer things tend to move more rapidly across the visual field, and distant things more slowly. Consider the view out the window of a moving train. Telephone poles beside the tracks whip by quickly; a house on the other side of a field moves more slowly, and a distant mountain slower still. Likewise, the textures of these various objects at vari-

ous distances also slide at various rates of speed across our retinas. And it is at the edges of these objects that these various rates of optical motion unfold. In this sense, edges are where the visual action is!

Edges are also those visual attributes we seem to attend to most when forming visual images. Our gaze constantly roams the visual world seeking out pertinent information about objects and surfaces around us. But in forming the optical image, our eyes are also engaged in small involuntary scanning flutters called *microsaccades*. At the edges of objects, this scanning yields information that is unique in the visual field. As our eyes scan back and forth across edges, the rods and cones on the retina receive information that oscillates back and forth, alternating between the information from the background to the information from the foreground object. Comparatively less information fluctuation attends those areas within objects or within uniform backgrounds. As might be expected, the areas where information oscillates the most, edges, are more important in forming the retinal image than those areas that do not change.

Figure 2.35 Macy's Day Parade (Photo: Bruce Lindsey).

Like a squeaky wheel that gets attention, edges initiate the retinal image.

Its Use in Drawing

On the basis of overlap, flats in theater stage sets and paper cutouts in children's pop-up books produce convincing spatial representations. It is for the same reason—the optical action at profiles—that simple line drawings achieve such a potent sense of the visual field.

---

[8] Given a stationary viewer, where gradients are not terribly obvious, readings of overlap function either according to prior knowledge of the shapes in the field or, lacking the former, according to the law of simplicity so valued by Gestalt psychologists. Both of these processes can be easily tricked.

[9] Motion parallax: Based on the apparent relative motions of objects at various distances from the observer when the observer is moving.

Figure 2.36a Line drawings: an instant of motion parallax. Rebecca Schultz.

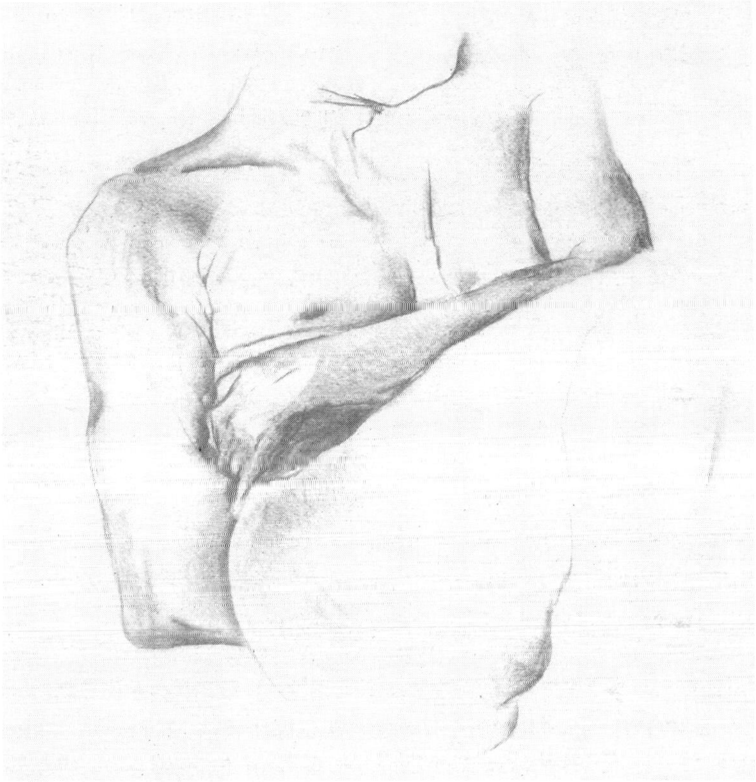

Figure 2.36b Consciously vary profiles. Patricia Clark.

It should not seem surprising therefore that line drawing is one of the very first ways that we learn to represent objects. In the sense that a profile establishes where something is and is not, line drawing offers the immediate utility of objectifying things.

Nevertheless, with line drawings it is important to prevent the outside edges of objects from becoming *too* dominant. A too-domi-nant profile flattens an image—much like the cutouts in the example of the pop-up books mentioned earlier. Instead, from time to time, let lines move away from the profile, and consciously vary their weight and character. Use a playful line. In Figure 2.36b, notice how Patricia has sometimes strongly emphasized the outside edge and at other times left it out altogether.

SHADE AND SHADOW (AND DISPARITY VISION)

Based on three-dimensional modeling of objects in light, shade, and shadow.

Its Signature

Gibson explains shading of objects in terms of densities of gradients on surfaces. Alone in his discussion of the secondary cues, his explanation of *shade* and *shadow* strikes me as somewhat obscure. But there is another explanation why shade and shadow seem to impart such convincing three-dimensionality to objects in the visual field, and this explanation is independent of Gibson's textural gradient.

Let me draw a comparison between shade and shadow and disparity vision.[10] Though differences between the two cues are obvious, their foundation is the same. They both depend upon the view from two distinct positions.

Disparity, or *binocular, vision* was the root of that wonderful toy of the nineteenth century, the stereoscope, that all of us have at some time seen on visits to the eye doctor. We look through a viewer at two adjacent photographs that are slightly offset, to differentiate the views from our two eyes. And voilà, the scene seems real in a way that no single photo can match.

Disparity vision was also the basis for the commercially unsuccessful (and headache-producing) 3D movies during the 1950s. I remember attending the *Charge at Feather River* (the Sioux versus the cavalry) sometime in the mid-50s and finding it absolutely necessary to duck the arrows that seemed to be flying out of the screen. The fact is that disparity vision does provide a powerful sense of the third dimension. How?

Disparity vision allows us to see, however slightly, *behind* things. Each eye can verify just what it is that is being hidden from the view of the other eye. Almost as a reprise of motion parallax, the second eye sees what would unfold behind the scene and at what rate, if only we were able to move our point of view from the position of the one eye to that of the other. It is, in effect, motion parallax without the need to move.

The comparison between shade and shadow and disparity vision is this: in the case of disparity vision, a second eye provides the second view; in the case of shade and shadow, the sun or some other source of illumination provides the information of the second view. By indicating from the point of view of the sun exactly what would be overlapped—shadow—and what

Figure 2.37 Shade and shadow can indicate surface shape and relief.

would be out of sight—shade (turned away from view)—it provides information that is every bit as potent as disparity vision. In fact, arguably, it is even more powerful. Under certain conditions, the sun at our backs and well to our left or right, the distance between the two sources and the resulting visual triangulation are great indeed.

Figure 2.38 Shade and shadow can indicate surface shape. Harvey Butts.

3. *Shade and shadow can indicate surface quality and relief.* A surface casting shade and shadow upon itself indicates roughness; a surface casting no shade and shadow upon itself indicates smoothness. An alpine landscape casts shadows into its valleys; the flat steppes of Russia cannot.

4. *Shadow can indicate shape.* The edge of a shadow forms a contour line on the object receiving the shadow. The form of that contour line gives information about the shape of both the object casting the shadow and the object receiving the shadow. A serrated knife casts a serrated shadow, even on a flat surface. A round object receives a rounded shadow, even from a straight-edged object.

5. *Shadow can indicate the relative position of objects.* An object that touches the shadow it casts also touches the surface receiving the shadow. An object that does not touch the shadow that it casts also does not touch the surface receiving the shadow. We know when a leaping man has left the ground. He disengages himself from his shadow.

Its Use in Drawing

Shade and shadow each inform us differently. In general, shade provides information only about surface; shadow provides information about both surface and location:

1. *Shade can indicate shape.* A gradual modeling from light to dark within a shaded surface indicates a rounded surface. An abrupt transition from light to dark indicates a faceted surface.

2. *Shade can indicate surface orientation.* The darkness of shading usually indicates the degree to which a surface is turned away from the light source.

---

[10] Disparity vision: Perception of depth based on the difference in the view from the two eyes.

SIZE PERSPECTIVE

Apparent reduction in size of objects at a greater distance from the observer.

Its Signature

Size perspective is based on the reduction of the projected sizes of objects and material textures with greater distance from the observer. It is optically related to *linear perspective*. Seen from the back of a train, the rails of a receding track converge into the distance. Likewise, at greater distance from the observer, the projected width between the rails also gets narrower, the telephone poles shorter, and the cows beside the track smaller.

With the textural gradient, Gibson freed size perspective somewhat from the necessity of perceptual learning. Prior to his work, size perspective was thought to be conditional, requiring knowledge of the real sizes of the objects in view in order to work. It was based on a comparison of sorts: a cow at a near distance versus a cow at a greater distance; the cow occupying the greater amount of surface in the visual image must be nearer. But for the cue to work, we had to know something about cows. With the textural gradient, an attribute of matter itself, perceptual learning is less necessary. Though certainly helpful, it is not absolutely required.

I once saw an amusing demonstration of size perspective on *Sesame Street* that illustrates the point. In this sequence, Grover came close to the camera and said, "near" and then ran off into the distance and said, "far." It was obvious to the viewer that the "nearer Grover" presented the larger image and the "farther Grover" the smaller. The sequence was skillfully presented, as I remember, so that no cues other than size perspective were in play. No ground surface was visible, nor was there any scenery that would lend a sense of linear perspective to the view. Furthermore, the fact of the flat television screen framing the view made the differences between the two projected sizes all the more compelling.

It might be assumed in this illustration that size perspective would be dependent on knowing Grover. Certainly knowledge did help. But independent of knowing Grover, as he ran away, his material textures also got smaller. His eyes and ears and the yarn strands of his fur and the intervals between them all got smaller.

Its Use in Drawing

One of the very first images that made me

Figure 2.39 Three depths defined by the projected sizes of three objects.

want to draw was called *The Preacher*, by Charles White (Figure 2.40). It shows a black preacher, invoking the word of God with his arms and hands thrust forward at the listener. It is a powerful image, made all the more powerful because White greatly exaggerates the projected sizes of the preacher's hands and forearms—with the result that they jab out of the canvas like a well-thrown punch!

plain was size perspective. And this was size perspective of a ticklish sort because the only thing whose sizes they could modulate were those small plants on the plain. How did they do it?

I went by one day and observed them at a fairly early stage. They had drawn a horizon line around the full circumference of the background painting, a length of some 30 feet. Pinned to this horizon line at eye-level height, like so many people on a clothesline, were human figures of all sizes. But while they were all different sizes, the proportions of these figures were carefully maintained. Then, day by day, plant by plant, at whatever height in the image they needed a bush or tuft of grass, the painters would simply dangle a human figure from the horizon line to that position on the ground. With the human figure, they had a ready proportioned scale, and knew exactly how large to paint each bush.

That is the more general use of size perspective: giving depth an extra push, whether by exaggeration of size or by skillful composition. But command of size perspective can be subtle as well, in particular in scenes where other cues, notably linear perspective, are absent.

Over a period of several months at the Carnegie Museum of Natural History in Pittsburgh, I once had the opportunity to watch two itinerant scene painters paint the background for a large diorama showing a view of the African savanna. The foreground had all sorts of animals—giraffes, zebras, antelope, and others—and surrounding trees and ground cover. In the middle-ground and background, the scene was intended to appear to extend out across a flat plain for miles and miles to distant mountains. Because the savanna is flat and relatively empty—just a few bushes and grasses—the primary cue these painters had available to show that

Figure 2.41 Cutouts of people, used to scale the textures.

ATMOSPHERIC PERSPECTIVE

Based on the effect of air on the color and visual acuity of objects at various distances from the observer.

Its Signature

Of the pictorial cues, atmospheric perspective is the most painterly. Its information varies as a condition of the context, its atmospherics, rather than as an absolute condition of the objects in a scene. It arises in the fact that the light reflected from distant objects must pass through more atmosphere to reach the observer than the light reflected from nearer objects. Two effects result:

1. *Distant objects appear bluer.* The materials of the intervening atmosphere (oxygen, water, and dust) tend to more effectively obscure the images of more distant objects, effectively supplanting them with their own reflected light, the blue color of our own familiar sky.[11]

2. *Distant objects appear less distinct.* In obscuring more distant objects, the intervening atmosphere is also intercepting the light reflected from those objects. The information from them is thus less complete. Less of it ever reaches the viewer. Bright surfaces appear grayer. Dark surfaces appear grayer. Sharp outline and detail are less crisp.

Figure 2.42 The nearer parts of the mill are more distinct, the distant hill less distinct.

Its Use in Drawing

For centuries, Western painters have mimicked the apparent "bluing" of distant objects merely by adding blue and reducing the saturation of local colors until objects acquire a soft blue-gray color in the distance. Fine Japanese screen painters have traditionally used watercolor washes to deliver a soft at-

- In describing the play of light on surfaces, give the nearer areas a greater range of contrast of value. In the foreground, make things that are darker very dark. Make things that are lighter very light. Then, as things recede into the distance, reduce the range of contrast between these extremes, in effect approaching middle-gray in the distance.

- In an effort to make the foreground appear sharper, use heavier, darker, and more precise lines for nearer objects. Lighten and soften lines of objects that are further away.

Figure 2.43 Aerial perspective. *Fur Traders Descending the Missouri,* George Caleb Bingham, oil on canvas, The Metropolitan Museum of Art, Morris K. Jessup Fund, 1933 (33.61).

mospheric depth to their landscapes. But there are also ways of representing aerial effects in tonal drawing and even line-drawing where color is absent. For drawing, the key issue is the reduction of visual acuity that occurs with greater viewing distance. Here are some tips:

[11] So distinct is the effect of this apparent "bluing" that geographic features are sometimes named for it. These usually are mountains or mountain ridges that tend to be seen from a greater distance: the Blue Ridge of Virginia, and Blue Mountain in Pennsylvania.

LINEAR PERSPECTIVE (AND PERSPECTIVE)

Based on the apparent convergence of parallel lines to common vanishing points with increasing distance from the observer.

Its Signature

Gibson finds perspective order in all environments, even in those with no straight lines and little obvious perspective content. Seen through Gibson's "textural gradient glasses," clouds in the distance near the horizon evidence intervals of foreshortening that seem every bit as orderly as a grid of ceiling tiles. Indeed, the textural gradient is just that: the material textures of the visual world, natural or artificial, seen as perspective order.

On the other hand, linear perspective is a kind of special case of perspective. It arises in circumstances where objects evidence parallel lines; where *x, y, z* right-angle coordinates are implied by the objects in the scene.

In Gibson's terms, perspective is a characteristic of the visual field rather than the "visual world." It approximates *how* we see, the retinal image, rather than *what* we see, the objects in the world before us. As a flat image, Figure 2.45 shows tracks converging, one big train and one little train, and trapezoidal passenger cars. But that is not what we perceive. We perceive tracks extending into the distance, a near train and a far train, and rectangular passenger cars.

As with this view, the potency of perspectives arises in their ability to capture a visual moment in a way that is specific to one individual, in one position in space, and in one moment in time — a powerful immediacy. I confess that the train in this painting still seems to rush out of the page at me now, much as it did when I first saw this same view as a child of 7.

There has always been a good deal of debate about perspective, dividing along two sides. Is perspective a truth of vision? Is it evident to greater or lesser degrees in everyone's environment and a universal fact of the visual image? Gibson would certainly answer yes. He is prepared to find perspective in all places, even the grains of sand of a desert.

Or is perspective something that is learned? Is it a case of life imitating art? Does the world seem to converge only after we have first made lines vanish to common vanishing points? Is perspective, in other words, a cultural artifact, an issue for the vi-

Figure 2.44 Gibson is prepared to see perspective order even in clouds near the horizon.

sion and representations of some, but not others? The approach in the first chapter of this book, "Engaging the Visual World," aligns partly with this last view. It presents the act of making marks as the initiator of drawing and, by implication, some aspects of seeing as well.

Figure 2.45 *Spirit of America.* Grif Teller.

We shall come to no resolution of this debate here. The issue is very much complicated by the fact that *how we see* and *how we represent what we see* are two very separate questions. For what it's worth, my own view takes a little from both sides. I think perspective is an absolute truth of the visual field, but only if we care to notice it. I have watched a sufficient number of students struggle with convergence to know that much about perspective must be learned. Be that as it may, this chapter does assume Gibson's views on perception and perspective. It treats perspective as an absolute truth of the visual field. But first: some history of perspective.

Its Use in Drawing: A Brief History through the Early Renaissance

The history of perspective is an interesting story in itself, beginning as it does with the ancient Greeks and having an impact even to the present day on the ways in which we construct artificial worlds in cinema and the computer. This history would be outside the scope of this book were it not for the impact it so obviously has on Gibson's conception of the visual world and, through that, on the approach to drawing in this chapter. I present this history briefly here to establish two understandings of perspective that are relevant to Gibson:

1. Perspective is based on an understanding of space that is universally applicable: that is, *x*, *y*, and *z* coordinates are extended everywhere.

2. Arising in that spatial conception, perspective makes the view of any one individual predictable within that space.

The Ancient Greeks and Romans

The ancient Greeks were the first to use perspective as a means to represent depth. In the fifth and sixth centuries B.C., their paintings of human figures evolved from a more rigid generic portrayal to one that used foreshortening and shading. They apparently reached a convincing level of "realism." Stories were told of Zeuxis, who painted grapes of such realistic appearance that even the birds pecked at them; and of Parrhasios, who painted drapes that caused people to try to draw them aside. It was also during the fifth century B.C. that the scene painter Agatharchos was credited with inventing perspective.[12] The Greeks' knowledge appears to have been empirical. As far as is known, they did not construct lines to central vanishing points. But they did at least appear to understand and use a kind of general convergence to construct quite convincing stage set designs.

[12] Blanshard, Frances Bradshaw. *Retreat from Likeness in the Theory of Painting* (New York: Columbia University Press, 1949), p. 15.

Figure 2.46 *The Battle of Issus,* ca. second to first century B.C., mosaic, 8'11" × 16'9½". Museo Archeologico Nazionale, Naples, Italy. Alinari/Art Resource, NY.

Figure 2.47 Sketch of wall painting, "Room of the Masks," ca. first century B.C., Palatine Hill, Rome.

The Romans subsequently copied the techniques developed by the Greeks—many of their artisans were Greek. It is largely through their artifacts that we have knowledge of the Greeks' earlier command of perspective. Images unearthed at Pompeii and Herculaneum in the eighteenth century show great understanding of both the convergence of parallel lines and the subtle foreshortening of human and animal forms. The mosaic in Figure 2.46, a copy of a Greek painting, dated from between the second and first century B.C., shows the *Battle of Issus,* Alexander the Great's victory over the Persians in 333 B.C.[13]

The scene presents the moment in which the tide of the battle turned, and Darius and the Persians began their flight. In the spirit of perspective, we have the feeling that we are there—the same immediacy of the moment that we recognize in the image of the train discussed earlier. The horses in the center and right are carefully foreshortened and racing along angular paths through the furious fight. Each combatant seems to occupy and defend a position on the battlefield.

Even more astonishing than the *Battle of Issus* is a mural discovered in 1961 on the Palatine Hill in Rome in the Room of the Masks and dated possibly from the first century B.C. If we trace the convergence of the edges in this scene and examine its foreshortening, we see a command of these issues that is every bit the equal of the early Renaissance masters. Did these painters in the ancient world know what is called "artificial" perspective? Did they know not just how to make perspectives based on observation, but on knowledge of optical projection as well? With this mural we have to conclude that they may well have.[14]

For reasons that are unclear, perspective vanished from use as the Roman Empire grad-

Figure 2.48 Sketch of *The Allegory of Good and Bad Government*, 1377–1379, Ambrogio Lorenzetti, Palazzo Publico, Siena, Italy.

Figure 2.49 Masaccio (1401–1428), *The Holy Trinity with the Virgin*. S. Maria Novella, Florence, Italy. Alinari/Art Resource, NY.

ually dissolved. The illusion of depth, so strong in the Roman images and even some early Christian images,[15] seemed to have been lost or become less necessary for the church and society as they subsequently developed.

Brunelleschi and the Renaissance Rediscovery of Perspective: A Universal and Continuous Order for Space

Perspective first reemerged in the work of some of the so-called proto-Renaissance painters. In the years between 1250 and 1350, a kind of "stage-set" perspective, reminiscent of images from Pompeii, is evident in a number of frescos: those in the Upper Chapel at

Assisi (attributed to Cimabue) depicting the life of St. Francis, Giotto's frescos in the Arena Chapel at Padua, and Lorenzetti's large mural for Siena's Palazzo Publico (town hall), to name a few. In these images, parallel lines do seem to converge, though never to consistent single vanishing points. Their technique shows receding lines slanting downward if they are above the horizon and upward if they are below the horizon.[16]

[13] Honour, Hugh and Fleming, John. *The Visual Arts: A History* (Englewood Cliffs, NJ: Prentice Hall Inc., 1982), pp. 146–153.

[14] Wright, Lawrence. *Perspective in Perspective* (London, Boston, Melbourne and Henley: Routledge & Kegan Paul, 1983), p. 38.

[15] *The Good Shepherd*, a mosaic at the Mausoleum of Galla Placidia in Ravenna dated A.D. 425 is an example of a late Roman Christian image that still made significant use of pictorial cues of depth.

[16] White, John. *The Birth and Rebirth of Pictorial Space* (Boston: Boston Book and Art Shop, 1967), pp. 23–85.

The first use of true convergent perspective is attributed to Brunelleschi sometime between 1416 and 1425,[17] and it is interesting that he used it as a simulation for a design proposal for the doors of the Baptistry in Florence. The first convergent perspective that still exists, *The*

Figure 2.50 *Bigallo Fresco,* Anonymous, fourteenth century. Panorama of Florence, detail from the *Madonna della Misericordia* fresco. Loggia del Bigallo, Florence, Italy. Orphanage of the Bigallo, Florence, Italy. Alinari/Art Resource, NY.

[17] Though Brunelleschi's image no longer exists, his biographer, Manetti, gives a detailed account. Brunelleschi, the designer of the great cupola at S. Maria del Fiore in Florence, had entered a competition for a new set of doors for the Baptistery opposite the church. He wanted to convince the reviewers that his proposal would be best, and he literally used mirrors. He positioned a mirror on the steps of S. Maria del Fiore such that the Baptistery was visible. Facing the mirror, he created a kind of peep-show demonstration. First he painted a perspective image of the Baptistery with his proposed doors on a solid plate. Then he cut a hole through the back of the painting. He positioned and aligned the painting so the mirror was viewed through that hole and so that his image of the Baptistery with his proposed doors was seen exactly superimposed over the scene of the background square in the mirror. Though the methods Brunelleschi used to create the actual painting remain unclear, the fact of the peep-hole and its obvious equivalence to the station point used in perspective construction give this image credence as the first artificially created perspective. I have relied on three accounts here: White, John. *The Birth and Rebirth of Pictorial Space* (Boston: Boston Book and Art Shop, 1967), pp. 112–121; Wright, Lawrence. *Perspective in Perspective* (London, Boston, Melbourne and Henley: Routledge & Kegan Paul, 1983), pp. 55–65; Edgarton, Samuel Y. Jr. *The Renaissance Rediscovery of Linear Perspective* (New York: Basic Books, 1975), pp. 3–15, 91–105.

Holy Trinity with the Virgin, was painted by Masaccio in 1425. It has been suggested that Brunelleschi showed him how to do it, but whatever the source, this painting is the first post-Roman image we have that uses convergence to single vanishing points. Others soon followed: in paintings by Paolo Uccello (1397–1475) and Piero della Francesca (1420?–1492) and in sculptural reliefs by Ghiberti (1378–1455) and Donatello (1386?–1466). Overnight—or so it must have seemed —the pictorial world had been remade.

How the World Seemed to Change

In his fascinating book, *The Renaissance Rediscovery of Linear Perspective,* Samuel Edgarton advances a provocative explanation of the nature of that change.[18] As polar opposites about that change, he discusses two topographical views of Florence that, roughly, straddle 1425, the year of *The Holy Trinity and*

[18] Edgarton, Samuel Y. Jr. *The Renaissance Rediscovery of Linear Perspective* (New York: Basic Books, 1975).

FIORENZA

Figure 2.51 *Map with a Chain,* eighteenth century reproduction of the *Catena Map of 1490.* Museo di Firenze com'era, Florence, Italy. Alinari/Art Resource, NY.

the Virgin. The first view is a detail from a fresco at the Loggia del Bigallo, painted circa 1350. The second is the *Map with a Chain* (named for its decorative chain border), an image of the city from 1480. Edgarton points out that, except for Brunelleschi's dome, there had been few physical changes in the city in the interval between the views—nothing physical, in other words, that might explain the obvious differences between these two presentations of Florence.

An inspection of the pictorial cues in the two views is revealing. Both clearly represent depth, but they use different cues to do it. Overlap seems to dominate the *Bigallo Fresco,*

but it is not the sort of overlap that yields a clear read of objects at various distances. Rather, the buildj109

ings in the scene seem to rush out at the viewer all at once. Upward position in the visual field is also evident; buildings lower in the picture are obviously nearer and the higher ones further. But because the ground is nowhere to be seen—the view is simply too crowded—it is not the sort of usage that yields much sense of where buildings are, relative to each other.

What does seem absolutely clear is our sense of the three-dimensionality of the buildings as individual parts (Edgarton uses

the term "depth shape"). Most are rendered in shade, and a Giottoesque convergence at their tops seems to create a unique viewing angle for each.

By contrast, the *Map with a Chain* presents a readable and continuous ground. While it is not a linear perspective, the view uses upward position in the visual field and some elements of size perspective with such detailed command that we have a real sense of where important buildings are located relative to each other. And we know much of the city's layout as well. We know that the city is built along both banks of the Arno. We know that the Uffizi Palace is near the river and that S. Maria del Fiore is further away. We could make similar positional statements about other buildings as well. Most important, because the background includes surrounding geographic features such as the mountains to the north and the hills to the south, we get a clear sense of where Florence is located in the world.

Does this mean that one view is more "real" than the other? Edgarton offers this observation. Each portrays something real about

Florence, but they show different realities. The *Bigallo Fresco* presents the "feel" of the city: the visual excitement it might have presented to an arriving visitor. The *Map with a Chain,* on the other hand, offers a sense of overview, a sense of the order of the whole.

Then Edgarton asks a provocative question: With which sense of the world would Columbus have ventured out across the Atlantic some 70 years after Brunelleschi in 1492? With that of the *Bigallo Fresco* or the *Map with a Chain?* With this question, Edgarton suggests a deeper meaning of perspective, one that goes beyond its optics and beyond its importance for making pictures. Perspective was, Edgarton suggests, a way of ordering the world in *x, y, z* coordinates, a way that would be universal and applicable everywhere. So useful would this spatial conception become that it would eventually emerge in the gridwork of Mercator maps in the 1600s as well, and make routine the navigation to distant lands as yet unknown. Gibson would have most certainly felt at home in such a spatial conception. It is the one from which his own understanding sprang.

How We Will Draw Perspectives

In the spirit of Gibson, at the outset we will try to derive our understanding of perspective by drawing things in which perspective order is implicit. To make things easier, we will draw buildings, which have repeated intervals of foreshortening and horizontal and vertical elements. However, somewhat in anticipation of

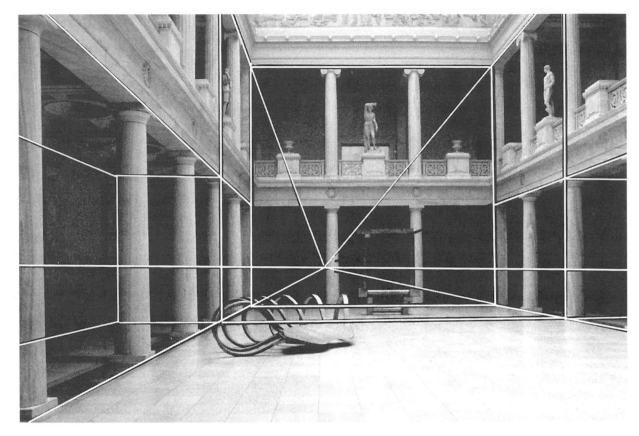

Figure 2.52 Develop an armature of convergent lines.

Chapter 3, we will also force geometric understanding into what we draw. We will do this to gain control over the perspective order that is already present in what we draw. Here are some general guidelines.

Observe the character of the view. Recognize the character of your view and its convergence at the outset. These factors will vary with your direction of view and position. If you are looking horizontally and parallel to the long wall of a space, that same long wall will appear to converge or vanish at a point directly opposite you, the point at which you're looking. On the other hand, if you're looking diagonally across a room at a corner, then the space will appear to generate two vanishing points on either side of your viewpoint. The heights of these vanishing points will also vary with your viewing location. If you're higher in the space, vanishing points will also be higher; if you're lower, they will also be lower.

Figure 2.53 Halve and double intervals of foreshortening.

Develop an armature of convergent lines. Note what the architecture offers you already: cornice lines, alignments of openings, and material joints. Using these lines, draw a host of converging guidelines that radiate out from the view's vanishing points.

Represent foreshortening by halving or doubling intervals. Look for an underlying geometric order in the surfaces of the space, and foreshorten that order. Look for a repetitive order. This may be a material texture, a structural framework, or a sequence of openings. Based on the diagrams in Figure 2.53, foreshortening can proceed in two ways from these elements:

- *Halving intervals (left side of space)*. Guess one large interval with an even number of parts, for example, four column bays. Using the diagonals of this interval, divide it into two halves. Using the same method continuously applied, subdivide these intervals into ever smaller units.

- *Doubling intervals (right side of space)*. Guess one small interval, for example, one column bay. Find the midpoint of an opposite side. Extend a diagonal from one corner of the interval through that midpoint, thus doubling the original interval.

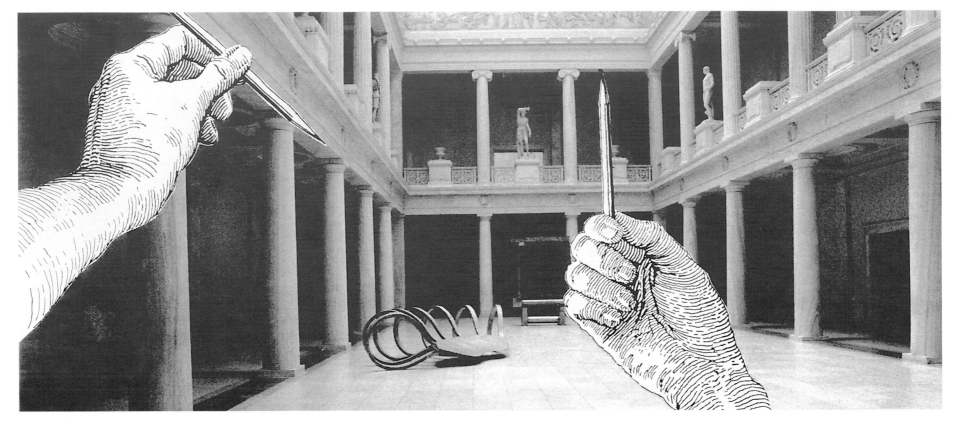

Figure 2.54 Measure projected angles and lengths.

Measure projected angles and distances on an assumed picture plane. Throughout the process of generating a perspective, you need to measure projected angles and lengths. In this way you incorporate the sense of the view from your location. Before beginning, remember that the projected angles and lengths you see before you will likely differ from the actual angles and lengths of the object you are drawing. What is in fact 90° will

likely not project as 90° in the perspective view; what is in fact a square probably does not project as a square. Whether measuring projected angles or lengths, you should imagine that you are viewing the scene before you through a large sheet of glass that has been placed perpendicular to your line of sight at a comfortable distance from you. You should conceive of making your measurements on that glass window:

- *Measuring projected angles (above left).* Use your pencil as a protractor of sorts. Place it over the optical angle you wish to measure, measure it (usually it makes sense to think of it as measured off the vertical or horizontal), and then transfer that angle to your drawing.

- *Measuring projected lengths (above right).* Use your pencil as a ruler of sorts.

Figure 2.55 A perspective should be developed around the geometry of the scene. Li Hang Wang.

Superimpose it over the distance in question and measure along its length. Then transfer that projected length to your drawing.

Develop the view directly over the geometric armature.[19] Having built the armature from the underlying geometry of the scene before you, develop the perspective of the space right over that armature. Think of it as hung over that armature, much as a curtain wall is hung on the structural frame of a building. Though the order of the framework has been derived from that architecture originally, let that framework now serve to give order back to the architecture as you draw.

[19] I want to acknowledge the contributions of Professor Bruce Lindsey and, indirectly through him, Professor Phil Grausman of Yale University, for my understanding of the geometric armature. A presentation of Grausman's teaching can be found in: Crit 15, *The Architectural Student Journal*, Summer 1985.

FREEHAND PERSPECTIVE 1
One-point interior view.

Go to a long, rectangular interior space that is characterized by repeated architectural intervals. Ideal spaces will have repeated structural bays. A church or an industrial warehouse would make good choices.

First derive the underlying geometry from the space. Begin with a freehand drawing of the geometry of the end wall. It should include information such as overall proportion, centerlines of columns, and heights of major elements, but it should remain abstract. You're drawing the underlying geometry of the end wall, not the wall itself. The lines should have the character of guidelines.

Then, locate a point on the end wall that is directly opposite your own position. Because you are looking parallel to the left and right side-walls of the space, this point will serve as the central vanishing point for the view. Draw a horizontal line through this point. This is the horizon line. It represents the horizon of the view as we would normally understand that term in daily life. It also represents the height of the viewer, your height, in the view.

Next draw a set of light lines radiating out from the central vanishing point. Within this set, emphasize those lines that are pertinent to the geometry of the space, cornice lines, string courses, tops and bases of openings, and the like.

Then foreshorten intervals of depth in the view. These might be structural intervals, such as column bays, or surface intervals, such as doors and windows. Use whatever is logical given your subject. Begin by guessing one interval. Then use one of the two methods outlined earlier, doubling intervals of foreshortening or halving intervals of foreshortening, and extend the intervals of depth of the armature out toward you.

Now that you have an abstract representation of a continuous space, draw the perspective right over the geometric armature. Try to retain a hierarchy of line-weights, with lighter lines representing the spatial armature and heavier lines representing the objects and surfaces in the space.

Figure 2.56 One-point perspective, where increments of foreshortening are guessed. Paul Miller.

Comments: *Making straight freehand lines is not natural, but it is necessary for perspective. Our arms are attached at our shoulders and, when we draw the long straight convergent lines that perspectives require, our arms tend to act like compasses — with the result that the lines have pronounced arcs. For the most difficult lines you can make things easier for yourself by rotating your drawing board so you can draw lines directly toward or away from your body, an easier motion to control.*

FREEHAND PERSPECTIVE 2
Two-point interior view.

Go to an interior space that is characterized by a strong diagonal direction of view and by repeated architectural intervals such as doors, windows, and structural bays. Draw the geometry of the space first. At an appropriate size, represent a major corner in the space with a light vertical line. At a height equivalent to your point of view, draw the horizon line across this vertical.

Figure 2.58 Kase Macosko.

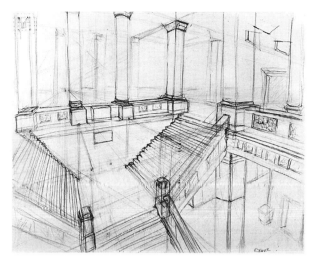

Figure 2.59 Edward Parker.

Figure 2.57 Jonathan Kline.

At points along the horizon line to the left and right of the corner, locate vanishing points for the two spatial axes of the space. Before you locate these, consider the orientation of your direction of sight relative to the space. There are two basic conditions: 1) If you are looking into the corner at an angle approximately 45° to either side, the two vanishing points will be approximately equidistant to either side of the corner. 2) If you are looking more nearly perpendicular to one of the walls, then the view will generate one vanishing point closer to the corner with which you begin and one further away. Figures 2.58 and 2.59 are examples of this condition.

Next, draw sets of light lines radiating out from the two vanishing points. Within these sets, emphasize those lines that are pertinent to the geometry of the space as it extends out toward you.

Now, guess and indicate one interval of depth in the view. This might be a structural interval, such as a column line, or a surface interval, such as a door or window. To complete the spatial framework, double intervals of foreshortening or halve intervals of foreshortening to extend the grid forward and to give it sufficient density. In general, more lines are better than too few lines.

As in the earlier one-point views, draw the objects and surfaces of the space right over the geometric armature.

Comments: *Figures 2.57, 2.58, and 2.59 are good examples of the kind of hierarchy of line-weights you should achieve. The idea is to distinguish the governing order: between the armature, which you make lighter, and the object itself, which you make darker.*

FREEHAND PERSPECTIVE 3
One-point view of stairs.

Stairs are interesting because of their three-dimensional complexity. No other architectural element so obviously addresses all three spatial axes. Furthermore, their sloping elements —banisters, handrails, and stringers—offer ready demonstration of the more general issue of vanishing points of slopes.

Start, as before, with a one-point framework derived from the space in which the stair is placed; represent the plan of the stair within that framework. Build the stair up from that plan, stair by stair, as an issue of rise over run. Better still, construct the height of a landing first and interpolate the risers between.

Observe that the stair's sloping elements imply a vanishing point. If your construction is reasonably accurate, banisters, handrails, and stringers will seem to converge naturally to a single point. If the stair is ascending up and away from you, that vanishing point should be directly above the central vanishing point. If the stair is descending down and away from you, it should be below the central vanishing point. Because the stair likely has the same slope whether ascending or descending, these two vanishing points should be equidistant from the drawing's central vanishing point.

Comments: *An important skill is learning to think and draw three-dimensionally. Something that fosters this kind of thinking is drawing transparently (as shown in Figure 2.60), drawing the stairs that are out of sight beneath the floor.*

Figure 2.60 Sung H. Kim.

Figure 2.61 Two-point view of stairs.

FREEHAND PERSPECTIVE 4
Two-point view of stairs.

To draw a two-point view of stairs, proceed in the same manner as you did with the one-point view. Begin with a projected plan of the stair and then build the stair up or down from that plan.

Comments: *The issue of the vanishing points for slopes gets more complicated in a two-point view. Depending whether they are ascending or descending, these points will still be equidistant above and below the vanishing point for the axis they parallel. But vanishing points for diagonals along axes that vanish far to the left or right will be further above or below than along axes that vanish closer to the center of vision.*

Figure 2.62 Slopes vanish above (or below) central vanishing points.

FREEHAND PERSPECTIVE 5
Perspective of octagonal forms.

Until now, most of the things we have drawn have lent themselves easily to perspective. The octagonal objects we will now address present a transitional set of challenges that will help when we address irregular forms later on in the book. In drawing these, we will need to generate diagonal surfaces.

Draw the subject from a direction that positions the object as a one or two-point view. As before, derive the armature first. Then generate the vanishing points for the diagonal edges of the object in relation to the rectangular grid. One way to do this is to represent a square in the projected plan. Then draw its diagonals and extend them to the horizon line, in effect extracting the vanishing points from the view where these lines cross the horizon line.

Figure 2.64 Katherine Bojsza.

Comments: *Though your understanding of the underlying construction needs to be very precise, from time to time, as in Figure 2.65, it is good to do these drawings fast, to invest them with the feel of the exercises in Chapter 1. Ultimately speed is an essential issue. If you cannot draw perspectives quickly, you will tend not to use them as a a tool in your design process.*

Figure 2.63 Octagonal forms generate multiple vanishing points (Photo: Howard Saalman).

Figure 2.65 Vincent Chew.

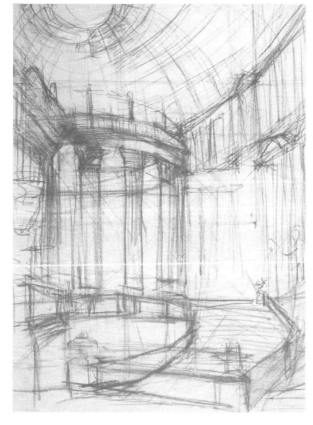

Figure 2.66 Ronni Fleisher.

Figure 2.67 Matthew Cross.

FREEHAND PERSPECTIVE 6
Stairs and faceted forms.

This exercise brings together most of the issues we have covered in freehand perspective construction so far: multiple vanishing points above and below the horizon line generated by slopes, as well as the multiple vanishing points generated by the diagonals we addressed in the most recent exercise.

The most important issue to keep in mind is that the stair, as it ascends or descends, also turns. We can understand it in perspective if we think of its plan generating diagonal cords that will vanish along the horizon line as the stair turns. Then, depending upon the slope, we can simply locate these vanishing points above or below the vanishing point for the cords.

Comments: *The best views that I know for this exercise are on the Spanish Steps in Rome, but if you can't afford a ticket to go there or you haven't a slide, then a spiral fire escape will do just fine.*

Figure 2.68 Ju-kay Kwek.

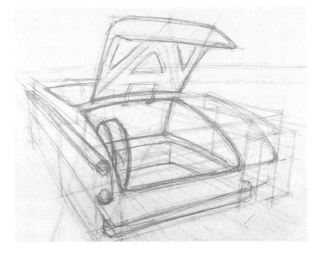

Figure 2.69 Matthew Cross.

objects that are round. Fifties-vintage cars are perfect for this exercise.

To draw the car as an issue of textural gradient in perspective, you need to map an x, y network into the car's surfaces. Do this by starting with a superimposed box drawn in perspective with vanishing points at the horizon line. Then draw sectional cuts (note the sectional cuts through the Studebaker in Figure 2.68) at various depths through the car and use these to generate the surface of the car.

Comments: *The drawing of the raised trunk in Figure 2.69 provided a great opportunity to apply knowledge of vanishing points of slopes, which was gained originally from drawing stairs. In this case, the vanishing point of the trunk had to be below the central vanishing point of the car.*

FREEHAND PERSPECTIVE 7
Rounded forms.

In preparation for the upcoming chapter, we will now take a more proactive approach to the geometry of our subjects. Such an approach becomes necessary when we draw

Figure 2.70 Use sectional cuts to generate round forms (Photo: Sarah Cooper).

Figure 2.71 Charles Elliott.

Figure 2.72 Jennifer Hanson.

Figure 2.73 Sloping roads generate vanishing points above (or below) the horizon line.

FREEHAND PERSPECTIVE 8
Views of hillside streets.

Though its geometry is less obvious, this exercise raises no new issues of construction. But because of its subject, it will bring us to the point where we can address the landscape in perspective, a subject we will take up in greater depth in the next chapter.

Find a sloping street that is lined with houses and that turns as it rises or descends. Proceed as you have in the previous exercise; that is, represent the slope first as a horizontal element. Generate vanishing points along the horizon line in alignment with the street as it turns. In doing this, you will be considering the street as a set of tangential lines. Then generate vanishing points for the sloping street above or below the vanishing points of these tangents.

Comments: *With its steep hillsides and geomorphic street layout, Pittsburgh has a wealth of sites such as those shown here. If you don't have such conditions nearby, photographs provide reasonable substitutes. Views of Italian hill towns or townscapes in the Greek islands would do. The key issue is that the scene should have streets that turn as they ascend or descend.*

MOVEMENT AND PERSPECTIVE

Without diminishing its value, Gibson's early work does seem to make vision almost passive. Once we consider the world to be already ordered, preordered we might say, vision seems reduced to a process of registering and recording, a role at odds with daily experience. The progress of Gibson's later work seemed to recognize this limitation. Beginning with *The Senses Considered as Perceptual Systems*, published sixteen years after *The Perception of the Visual World*, he gave much greater weight to the role of movement in visual perception. By the time of his last work, *The Ecological Approach to Perception*, vision emerged as a much more dynamic sense of a perceiver who is constantly interacting with the environment.

Clearly then, movement is an issue for perspective. Perspective presents the view from a fixed position and looks in only one direction, and we must acknowledge that we seldom view the world this way for long. Most of the time, we are moving while we look. As a conclusion to this section on perspective and Gibson, and as a parallel to the progress of Gibson's later work, I want to present several ways perspective might acknowledge movement. As this issue has been central in my own work, I will use my own drawings as examples.

Figure 2.74 *Holt and Barry Streets,* by the author, 80" × 112" charcoal on paper on canvas. Senator Heinz History Center mural (1992–1993).

A Sculptor's Assignment

Years ago, when I was studying architecture, my drawing teacher, Kent Bloomer, now at Yale, gave my class a strange assignment. He asked us to draw everything inside our studio and everything outside as well. Kent is a sculptor, and I have come to think that his assignment had much to do with his trade. As a sculptor, he brought a natural skepticism about drawing to the class. Accustomed to considering his work in the full round and from all aspects, he distrusted the value of perspective for its limitation to one direction of view and one standpoint.

Eventually, Kent's assignment led me outside to draw Pittsburgh, where I found a dynamic landscape whose steep and twisting slopes presented multiple directions of view. It made me look upward while I drew. It made me look downward, too; it made me turn and move along the street—all while I drew.

Figure 2.75 *St. Johns and McCardle Roadway,* by the author, 48" × 96" charcoal on paper on board (1998). Private collection.

Drawing Pittsburgh

I have drawn Pittsburgh for many of the years since, and Kent's assignment has meant a career for me. I have done civic murals and smaller images, all built on the more dynamic sense of vision that was implicit in his assignment. For the purpose of loosening somewhat the shackles of perspective, I want to give examples of some of the techniques that I've found useful in drawing Pittsburgh and, with them, some advice:

- Draw what you *can't* see—what's around the corner, behind the house.
- Let the vanishing points slide a little.

Figure 2.76 This drawing shows where to begin. Note how the hall at the left is turned slightly. In effect, the view is really two views: a two-point view toward the left and a one-point view down the hall. Toshi Oki.

When Order Is Imposed

Drawing as Imposed Order

WHEN ORDER IS IMPOSED

A Trip to Bryce Canyon

In summer 1989, I took a week-long sketching trip to Bryce Canyon in southern Utah. I had hit a low point in my own work, and I thought drawing for an extended period in that very rich and three-dimensional environment would give me a spark for a new direction. What happened to my own work as a result of my visit to Bryce is outside the scope of this book, but something I learned there about the process of drawing is central.

Bryce Canyon exists at a very potent level of abstraction. People have described it as an immense "dribble-castle" spread over a 50-square-mile area. It is a playground for what psychologists call "projective imagery," that very interesting process of attaching meaning to something while perceiving it in error. A simple example would be looking out an airplane window and seeing the face of Abe Lincoln in a cloud formation.[1]

In Bryce Canyon, people look at rock formations and see all sorts of things. Some see people—one spire is named Queen Victoria. I tend to see architectural imagery, such as castles and gothic churches. Others see beasts and animals. The canyon is a bigger-than-life-size "Rorsach test" in stone.

Order Originates with the Viewer

For our purposes, what is interesting about projective imagery is the direction of its as-

Figure 3.1 Bryce Canyon, Utah, a playland for projective imagery.

signment of meaning. Meaning originates with the viewer and is directed at what is seen. This is the opposite of what we have considered in the previous chapter. There, with Gibson's help, we assumed that order already exists in the environment around us. As it concerned perspective, we keyed on linear details such as cornices and column intervals, and through

them were able to see, read, and re-create the perspective order implicit in the building we were drawing. Though at times we imposed some geometric constructions, these only had the purpose of clarifying order that we believed was already there. But with the example of Bryce Canyon, we see evidence that order can also originate with the beholder.

It occurs to me that what I was doing that summer with these sketches was something parallel to the mechanism of projective imagery, which I described earlier. Yes, I was responding to what I was drawing. But the order I was using, the x, y, z coordinate system, was mine. It originated with me, not the rocks I was drawing. Perhaps we use perspective in this way more often than we think, not just with rocks in a place as strange as Bryce Canyon, but even with buildings where perspective seems obvious.

Figure 3.2 Author's sketch at Bryce Canyon, Utah: imposing perspective on a scene.

Just as a matter of technique, during my week in Bryce, I often found I had to do more than just observe its stone formations in order to draw them. There were some formal clues already in the stonework to be sure. The stone in Bryce is sedimentary. It's limestone with various amounts of iron, and owing to erosion it has very pronounced horizontal lines. But I found all these clues insufficient to understand the three-dimensional order of what I was drawing. Often I had to use x, y, z coordinate constructions like the one shown in Figure 3.2 in order to fully grasp shapes. It was easier when I forced these networks onto the formations and used them to understand the natural conditions.

[1] Projective imagery was first studied in depth by Gestalt psychologists. Considering that they emphasize the role of preexisting schemata in perception, it is a central mechanism for them. In a loose sort of way, this chapter does align with Gestalt psychology. Order is considered as originating with the viewer. However, the parallel should not be taken too far. There is no argument here that perspective is a schema with which viewers are born.

Perspective: A Chicken and Egg Issue

In the previous chapter, I hinted that perspective might be more than just an observable fact of the environment, and I suggested that there is something of a chicken-and-egg issue that surrounds the subject. Does perspective exist as observable perceptual law for all to see, or does the world seem to appear in perspective only after we first understand the concept?

There is an interesting parallel to this issue—perspective as observable fact versus perspective as imposed construct—in the history of its development during the early Renaissance. Like myself in Bryce Canyon, the early perspectivists also ran into a problem that they simply could not solve through observation alone.

Alberti's Invention of the Station Point and Picture Plane

Just as we have done with all our perspective constructions so far, the early perspectivists were also basing their determination of foreshortening on guesswork. In views with single vanishing points, they knew how to make lines recede to common points. They used a system called *Pavimenti*, meaning floor tiles. They laid out pictures as gridworks on the floor of the view at the start. They simply measured equal increments along the view's base, and converged lines through these intervals to common vanishing points.

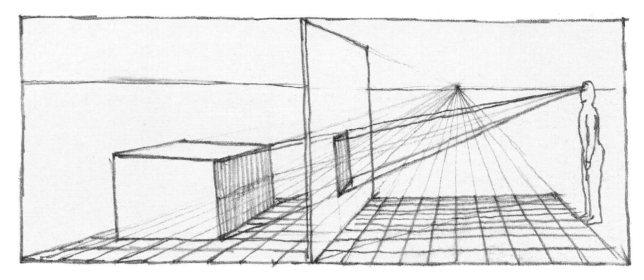

Figure 3.3 Alberti's visual pyramid.

But they were left with guesswork to determine the projected depths of the tiles as they receded into the scene. Various proposals were put forth, some based on observation and some on arithmetic systems. A popular standard was to reduce successive intervals by thirds. But the problem with all of these methods was that none resulted in straight diagonals.

Leon Battista Alberti (1404–1472) provided a solution. Alberti was the very model of a "Renaissance man." Mathematician, architectural theoretician, and architect, he wrote *Della Pittura*, which forms the first codification of perspective, in 1435. Alberti scorned the various empirical and arithmetic practices of the day, and his treatise on perspective did

solve the problem of the diagonal. But that result was only an effect, a check of sorts for the accuracy of his methods.[2]

He presented a general understanding of the underlying optics of perspective based on the view from an individual observer. To model perspective, he proposed something he called the "visual pyramid." Points on objects were projected through a picture plane to the viewer, thereby generating an image, which bore a measurable relationship to the object in the picture. His construction served to unify for the first time the relationship between the objects in a scene, the picture plane, and the viewer.[3]

Alberti's stance was much more proactive than his contemporaries. Not content, as they

Figure 3.4 Depiction of Alberti's understanding of the picture plane. Dürer, Albrecht (1471–1528). *Artist drawing a reclining nude.* Engraving. Location not indicated. Foto Marburg/Art Resource, NY.

were, to base his understanding on observation alone, he imposed a unified construction upon the world first, and it was with that order that he observed the objects in the world.

What does this mean for us? In our approach to perspective so far, we, like Alberti's contemporaries, have used observation alone. Alberti's work requires that we no longer think of objects in isolation—the images of the individual buildings seen from individual directions in the *Bigallo Fresco* from the previous chapter come to mind. Instead, we must consider (and draw) objects as part of a larger spatial conception. We have to think of the continuous perspective space first and then place the objects in it, rather than the other way around.

Consider foreshortening. Consider the horses in the mosaic, the *Battle of Issus* (discussed in the previous chapter), and the spatial conception that might have led to their being so accurately foreshortened. It was one that, from the outset, required the original Greek painter to consider the horses as parts of the larger order of the whole picture: as participants in the ongoing battle arrayed on the field. Understood in that larger context, the horses had to occupy space and hold spatial relationships relative to the other combatants. It was as participants in that greater

whole that they were foreshortened, not as individual horses.

On the Wings of Uccello

With respect to my experience in Bryce Canyon, and in light of Alberti's work in perspective, one of the most interesting early perspective painters was Paolo Uccello (1397–1475). Uccello loved perspective, indeed so much so that he was severely criti-

---

[9] Alberti's method of one-point perspective entered common practice. This method, today called the magic method, can be used for quick freehand views. It is discussed in detail in Appendix A.

[3] White, John. *The Birth and Rebirth of Pictorial Space* (Boston: Boston Book and Art Shop, 1967), pp. 121–126.

Figure 3.5 *Battle of Issus* (detail). Mosaic. Museo Archeologico Nazionale, Naples, Italy. Alinari/Art Resource, NY.

cized by his contemporaries for being too much in love with it. To my eye, some of his most interesting works are those in which he seems to get some things in true perspective and some things not. His painting the *Battle of San Romagna* (ca. 1450) is a mural-sized image in several panels, whose background landscape seems almost a throwback to earlier proto-Renaissance painters. Its interesting shifts in scale and somewhat upturned surface present a wonderful foil for the foreground. With that foreground, in particular its ground surface, Uccello is fully in tune with the latest perspective tricks of his day, and he takes perspective even further than his contemporaries.

Not content to merely record the events of the battle in perspective, he intervened with perspective into the event itself. The poor fellows who perish in this battle do not merely die. They die in perfect one-point perspective convergence! And dutifully, for Uccello's purposes, they apparently have the good sense in their last moments of life to cast down their weapons as well—once again in perfect one-point convergence.[4]

Uccello—Piero della Francesca (1420?–1492) is another—is credited by some as being among the first to move beyond Alberti's grid system to a scheme of projecting perspectives from plans and elevations, the procedure that is presented in conventional form in Appendix A of this book.[5] What is certain is that over the course of his

Figure 3.6 Uccello, Paolo. *The Battle of San Romano,* ca. 1450, National Gallery, London.

life, Uccello developed an extraordinary facility for understanding odd-shaped objects in perspective, even objects that are not immediately recognizable for their perspective content at all. Two of his most remarkable drawings show a chalice and a *mazzocchio,* a hollow ring of wickerwork used for a Renaissance headdress.[6] Looking at these we are immediately struck by Uccello's understanding of the order that would underlie Mercator's (1512–1594) maps with their longitude and latitude. He seems to recognize

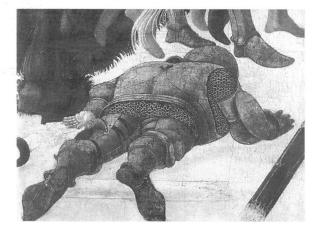

Figure 3.7 Uccello, Paolo. *The Battle of San Romano,* ca. 1450 (detail), National Gallery, London.

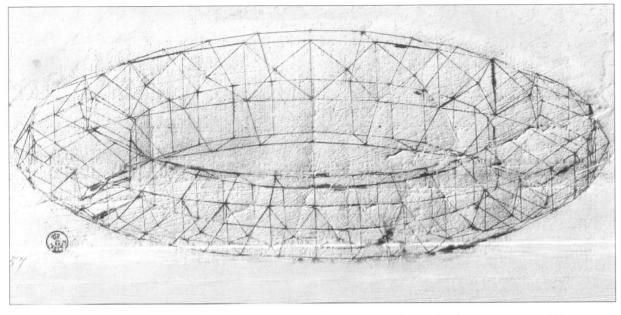

Figure 3.8 Uccello, Paolo (1397–1475). *Perspective study of a mazzocchio.* Uffizi, Florence, Italy. Alinari/Art Resource, NY.

Figure 3.9 Uccello, Paolo (1397–1475). *Perspective study of a chalice.* Uffizi, Florence, Italy. Alinari/Art Resource, NY (image modified for clarity).

the utility of casting an *x, y* coordinate network over a complicated object in order to define its form.

But the key to these constructions is their transparency. In both, Uccello uses sectional cuts through the objects to generate their appearance. The drawing of the mazzocchio uses 32 different views of a hexagon rotated through the form. The chalice shows horizontal contours that go completely around it. As a result, we feel as if we can look through the chalice to its backside. For Uccello, it is not only space that is continuous, but surface as well. And he uses the one to get to the other: ordering the backside with the same understanding as the front, and using sections in perspective to mediate between the two.

The Exercises

In this chapter, we will approach what we draw in the proactive spirit of Alberti and Uccello. We shall assume that drawing is a process of imparting order to the things that we draw. Yes, we will respond to what is already present in an object, but in the final analysis we will impose perspective order onto whatever we draw. We shall do so—ready or not—whatever the nature of the things we draw, be they houses, hills, or kumquats.

[4] Wright, Lawrence. *Perspective in Perspective* (London, Boston, Melbourne and Henley: Routledge & Kegan Paul, 1983), pp. 70–74.

[5] *Ibid.*, pp. 70–79.

[6] *Ibid.*, p. 73.

IMPOSING PERSPECTIVE 1
Imposing perspective on the figure.

Before moving out into the landscape, where forms are less accepting of the imposition of perspective, we will impose perspective first on something more familiar: the human figure. We will build on an earlier exercise from the first chapter: *drawing the figure with straight lines only* (pg. 24).

The model should take a pose in which elements of the pose are foreshortened. Reclined or lateral poses are usually good. Standing poses are appropriate only if viewed from close in, where, owing to a steeper viewing angle, foreshortening and convergence are more obvious. Poses with twisted elements will also work.

With line as the basic element, draw the pose or elements of the pose as an object made of planes. Begin by identifying the cardinal planes in the pose: front, side, and back. Try to visualize the locations where corners might exist between these planes: where side would meet back, where front would meet side, and so on. After you identify these planes, try to think of each as having a singular spatial orientation and related convergence to vanishing points.

Exaggerate convergence. Extend lines beyond the figure, to establish the flow of groups of lines to shared vanishing points. In the spirit of Uccello, and to visualize the figure in the third dimension, don't draw only

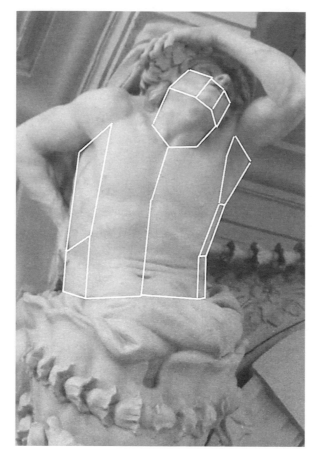

Figure 3.10 Imposing cardinal orientations on the figure.

Figure 3.11 Yella Lee.

what is visible; use sectional cuts to draw what is out of sight as well.

Figure 3.12 John C. Ferri.

Figure 3.13 Eric Watts.

Figure 3.14 Yella Lee.

Comments: *One model I often use has a unique pose: seated, he tucks his legs under his body and leans back until his shoulders touch the bench. He is amazingly limber, and I would not advise many to try this pose. But it does have the happy effect for this exercise of making his chest appear to have facets like a bent or folded plate.*

One note about defining planes on the object: keep them simple. It is better to have only a few planes and to retain a clear sense of their spatial orientation than to have a lot. If your drawing starts to resemble Spiderman, you're drawing too many planes. Also in the spirit of keeping things simple, I find it helpful to use shading to clarify facets and sectional cuts.

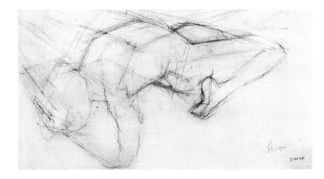

Figure 3.15 Neil Stroup.

Figure 3.16 Develop a reference plane. Build the land over it.

IMPOSING PERSPECTIVE 2

Imposing perspective on urban landscapes.

This exercise is similar to the one at the conclusion of Chapter 2, *views of hillside streets* (pg. 111), but with one critical difference. There we read the slopes using the buildings in the scene as a sort of crutch. We defined slopes in terms of their descent and ascent off of horizontals, which were articulated by the architecture. Here we generate the landscape directly.

Find an interesting uphill or downhill scene that has roadways and stairways set in the landscape. It might have a few buildings, but it should be a setting with a good deal of visible ground surface.

Begin by using the horizon line to construct a gridded continuous horizontal plane that extends back in space from where you are standing. This plane will serve as a reference plane, a "datum" of sorts. Use it to locate the

Figure 3.17 Kelly Leigh Williard.

roads and steps as projected plan shapes upon it. Then build the sloping roadways, steps, and ground surface up or down from this plane. Think of these elements in much the same way as you considered stairs in the previous chapter. Each portion of sloping road should generate a vanishing point along the horizon line in accordance with its plan orientation, and one above or below the horizon line in accordance with its inclination. Use these sloping elements to construct sets of sectional cuts through the ground in perspective.

Comments: *The key to this exercise is keeping the construction transparent. Note how in Figure 3.17 the plan of the road is visible beneath the ground.*

Figure 3.18 Ju-kay Kwek.

Figure 3.19 Jarrett Pelletier.

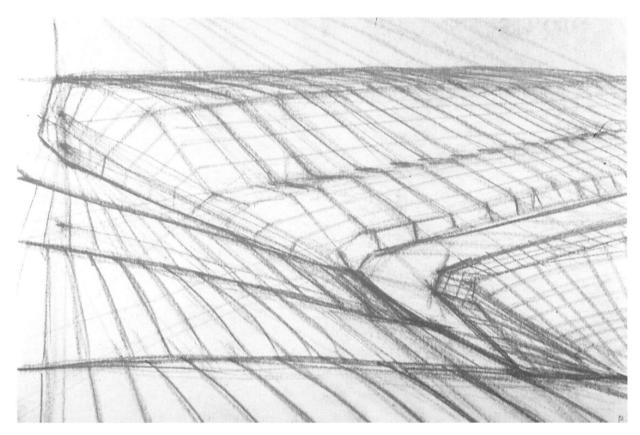

Figure 3.20 Susan Bhang.

Figure 3.21 Golf courses with their artificial forms are ideal for imposing perspective.

IMPOSING PERSPECTIVE 3
Imposing perspective on the rural landscape.

Find an interesting uphill or downhill rural scene. The more natural the condition and the fewer the number of artificial elements in the scene the more challenging the drawing will be.

As in the previous exercise, begin by projecting a continuous plane into the scene, then build a simplified version of the groundscape up or down from this plane. Consider orientations of sloping surfaces in much the same manner as you thought of the roadways in the previous exercise. Think of them as having vanishing points above and below the horizon line in accordance with their orientation and slope.

Figure 3.22 Esther I. Chen.

Figure 3.23 David Quintana.

Comments: *Draw sets of sections through the landforms in an effort to coordinate information developed in plan with information about elevation. You should consider this exercise as one in which you are constructing the outward surface appearance of the ground by generating its underlying geometry.*

A subject with a middle level of difficulty is a scene in a park that has a pathway or two. For the artificiality of its landforms and its openness, a quite wonderful subject is a hilly golf course. Golf courses are good even in flat environments because even there they will have bunkers and raised greens that are well suited to this exercise.

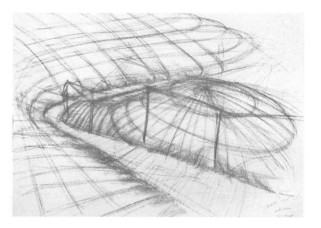

Figure 3.24 Missi Nickle.

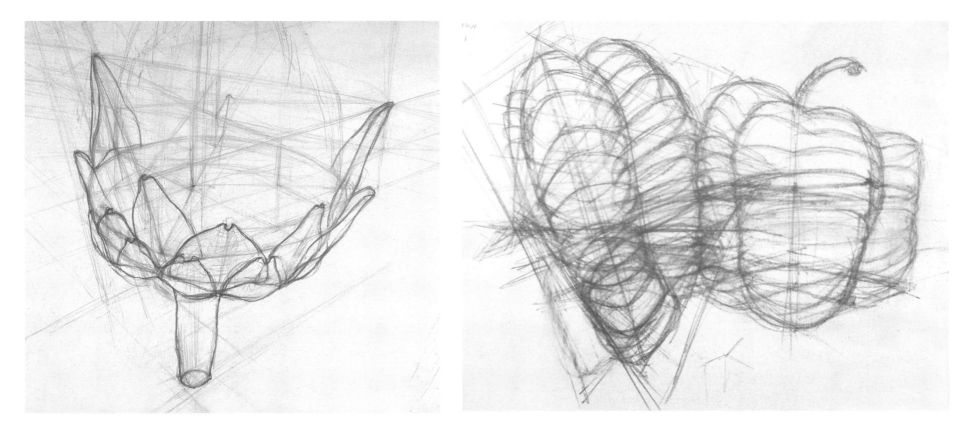

Figure 3.25 Jonathan Kline.

Figure 3.26 Missi Nickle.

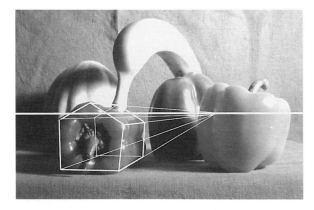

Figure 3.27 Build an armature using sectional cuts.

IMPOSING PERSPECTIVE 4
Imposing perspective on a still life.

Build an interesting architectonic still life out of fruits and vegetables. Items with interesting geometrical features will be best. Bananas, bell peppers, apples, and zucchini squashes will be good because of their facets, as will pineapples because of their surface textures.

Construct the still life as a kind of miniature architectural scene that you anticipate viewing from a low vantage point. Be imaginative! Span one of the bananas from one element to another. Cut open the bell pepper to reveal its inside. Do as much as you can to make the still life seem like a miniature world.

View the scene from a low vantage point and begin by drawing a gridded continuous

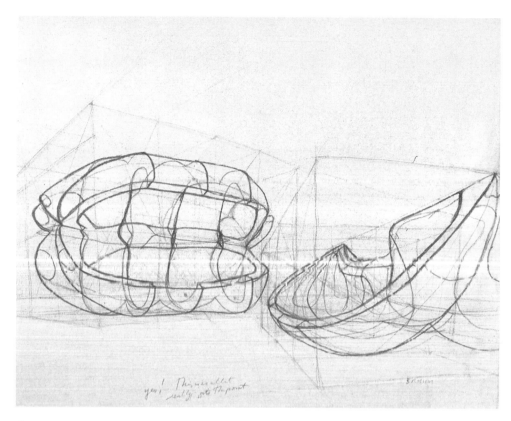

Figure 3.28 Tim Brochu.

Figure 3.29 Matthew Cross.

ground plane back to the horizon line—the table on which you've placed the objects. As in the previous exercise, lay out the objects in plan first. Try to visualize sectional cuts penetrating the various objects in the scene. Use these to build the objects up from the ground plane.

Comments: *It is good to be playful with this exercise and to make it fairly complex. Though buildings may have more details, their geometry will be no more complex than what you encounter with these fruits and veggies. Take heart from doing a good job with this exercise. If you can draw something this complex, you can draw most anything!*

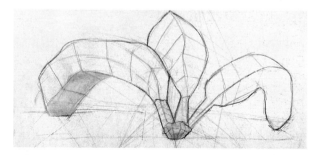

Figure 3.30 Lillie Liu.

LIGHT AND DARK AND COLOR

Study of Relationships, not Absolutes

We have already addressed one depth cue, linear perspective, in the proactive spirit of this chapter. Now we will turn to another, shade and shadow, and treat it in the same way. Rather than just reading from the environment around us, we will force our own interpretations into what we draw. Our work with shade and shadow and, more generally, light and dark will lead us ultimately to color.

The study of light and dark and color is a study of relationships, not absolutes. Daily life offers frequent relational perceptions. Something may appear tall to us, but this perception always implies a relationship to something else. I am 6 feet tall. That is an absolute measure of sorts. But it is not a perceptual one. My perceived height can vary in accordance with my context. I would look tall and lanky next to jockey Eddie Arcaro and undeniably short next to basketball player Wilt Chamberlain.

Such is the case with many properties of light and dark and color. In absolute terms, a fully saturated[7] red is a middle-dark color. In a continuum of fully saturated swatches of color (yellow, orange, green, blue, and violet) red would rank about in the middle in value,[8] lighter than blue and violet, slightly darker than green, much darker than yellow and orange.

Despite this absolute measure of the value of red, we can perceive the same red

Figure 3.31 Coca-Cola® red is both lighter than the soft drink and darker than the graphic.

as either dark or light depending upon its context. Placed against a warm black background, such as the liquid in the bottle, the familiar Coca-Cola red can appear positively luminous, but on the bottle in the context of the white graphic, the very same red will look dark. Did the darkness of the color change between the one circumstance and

the other? No, what did change was the context and, with it, our perception. Such relational judgments will be at the heart of our approach to light and dark and color drawing.

Sharpen and Emphasize Contrasts

In looking at light and color, it is important to

Figure 3.32 Hans Hillmann. Illustration from *Fliegenpapier*.

Figure 3.33 Hans Hillmann. Illustration from *Fliegenpapier*.

search out, sharpen, and even exaggerate contrasts. Contrast is a matter of both composition and conception, and it can be used to underscore both depth and content.

Some of my favorite drawings of light and dark are by German illustrator Hans Hillmann, who presented a beautifully illustrated version of Dashiell Hammett's *Fly Paper,* a gangster story set in San Francisco.[9]

Throughout his book, Hillmann artfully exploits the contrast of juxtaposed areas of light and dark. Indeed, like a film noir director, he arranges and choreographs his scenes as layers of overlapping light and dark profiles, with great cinematic effect. The two scenes shown here, the before and during of a barroom brawl, have many adjacencies of light and dark that underscore the stiff ten-

sion of the moment before the fray and the chaos that ensues. In the first scene, the bald bartender apprehensively stands out, along with the labels of his liquor bottles: white against the dark wood. The waitress furtively stands between the potential adversaries, her hair dark against the light bar, her white arm rigid against the dark base, and her ankle a stiff dark against the bright floor. The white of the table and bar in combination present a tense zigzag space that suggests that something has to "give."

What gives is a donnybrook of dark against white, white against black, with arms and legs and torsos flailing every which way.

As we proceed with the subject, we will also discover that light and shadow offer important information about the surfaces and shapes of objects. As we noted in Chapter 2's discussion of depth cues, light casts shadows on objects and models their forms in shade. The contours of these shadows and shades reveal the forms of the objects on which they are cast.

We will start with this observation and with a highly simplified approach.

---

[7] Saturation: The amount of a particular hue in a color.

[8] Value: The measure of the lightness or darkness of a color.

[9] *Fliegenpapier* is the German translation of Dashiell Hammett's *Fly Paper,* illustrated by Hans Hillmann (Frankfurt am Main: Zweitausendeins, 1982), pp. 22, 34.

LIGHT AND DARK 1

Imposing two values on the figure.

Ink, ¼" brush, bond paper

In working with value (light and dark), we're going to start simple and then proceed to greater complexity. Initially, we will consider only two values, then four, and gradually expand the number, learning in the process to juggle more and more variables.

Have the model take a pose under fairly harsh light. Adjacent to a window would be a good condition. Consider the surface of the model as either dark (black ink) or light (blank page). Whatever the range from light to dark in the scene, proactively impose the order that it *must* be either light or dark. With your black or white filter, no other values are possible.

Begin by squinting your eyes as you look. You will find this serves to simplify the range of light, and allows you to focus somewhat more easily on the shapes of areas. Then use your brush to develop the darker areas from their centers out. Avoid outlining areas. Start from the centers of the darker areas and gradually enlarge them. Consider simultaneously both their shapes and those of the adjacent white areas.

Make your rendition of dark versus light serve your pictorial intent. You are engaged in an immense simplification of the scene, and how you simplify will either help to clarify the scene or obscure it. Make it do what you want

it to. In the spirit of Hillmann's drawings, force an interpretation that yields overlapping edges and that emphasizes contours.

Comments: *I want to get at the essence of this exercise with a cautionary note and a comparison to sculpture. In this exercise, you cannot reclaim the white space of the page. Once you've made an area black, it's black. Therefore, at the outset, undersize the areas of black. Make them smaller than you think they should be and be content to nudge the drawing along.*

White space is the most critical material you have. For you it is what stone is for a sculptor. At the outset, you have a lot of it — you have a white page; the sculptor has a large stone. You both proceed by taking away from what you have. You blacken it out; the sculptor chisels it away. Just as the sculptor has to be careful not to chisel away too much stone, lest he remove what ultimately should be a nose or a finger, you must take care lest you remove too much light.

The comparison applies to the end game as well. When the process works, what is left over in both cases takes on a figural meaning. The sculptor

Figure 3.34 Katherine Ruffin.

is left with a stone that becomes a human being, and you are left with white page that becomes light. And each material, stone or white page, takes on that figural meaning when just the right amount of each is left.

Figure 3.35 Riita Vepsalainen.

ment you'll need to use. As you mix your colors, evaluate them with a set of adjacent swatches to test the value intervals between them.

Then draw the scene with these four values. As you work, try to shape the areas of color in such a way that they suggest the form of the figure by creating articulate contours on its surface.

Comments: *As was the case in the previous exercise, you need to consider the white paper as the key material in the process. Give it up carefully. The drawing will work when you reach the point at which the white space suddenly looks like the light on the surface of the object.*

In this exercise, you can work either from light to dark or dark to light. However, I find it easiest to start in the middle, by using the ocher first. Assuming you have mixed the colors so they dry reasonably quickly, you can then lay the umber and black over top, and come back and refine the break-line between ocher and white at the end.

LIGHT AND DARK 2

Imposing four values on the figure.

¼" brush; black, umber, ocher watercolor; watercolor paper (low-quality okay)

By using four values, this exercise increases the subtlety of range available. However, you still need to be attentive to where you make the break between each of the colors. As in the previous exercise, you want the break-line contours between the colors to work for you.

Mix the three colors, darkest (black), dark (umber), light (ocher) so that, together with the white page, they yield an even set of intervals from dark to light. The amount of pigment you mix into the colors, how watery you leave them, relates to the paper you're using. The less absorbent the paper, the more pig-

LIGHT AND DARK 3

Chiaroscuro: Working from the middle out.

Black, white prismacolor, gray charcoal paper

In the two previous exercises, on account of the media used, you started at the lighter end of the spectrum: the state of the untouched paper at the outset of the exercise. Your analysis proceeded likewise, in a parallel direction from light to dark. Because of the background gray paper you will use for this exercise, your starting point now will be the middle of the spectrum.

Choose a piece of architectural sculpture that has a variety of articulate shapes of dark and light, and that has a sufficient range of value from dark to light. Working with white and black prismacolor on gray charcoal paper, describe the full range of value of the surface of the sculpture. As in previous exercises, try to proactively interpret the shapes of the areas of dark and light so that they suggest form.

Work in a manner that builds on the previous exercises. Simplify at the outset and then proceed in an iterative manner. Start with just three values: white, gray paper, and black. Then expand these to five, all the while being attentive to the shape of the gray space, which in this exercise functions much as the white space did in the previous exercises, as one of the colors in the palette.

Figure 3.36 Teri Tsang.

Figure 3.37 Cynthia Kress.

Comments: *This is an exercise you do not want to hurry. Since you cannot easily erase the prismacolor from the paper, you need to "hedge your bets," so to speak, by committing only gradually to the range of value. The analogy to playing poker is apt. Faced with an opponent you've never played before at an evening's game, you adopt a wait-and-see approach. First you watch how your opponent plays. You need to know your opponent's strengths, weaknesses, and tendencies before you bet your house. Drawing with values is a similar juggling act. Proceed gingerly.*

Figure 3.38 Kase Macosko.

Figure 3.39 Jaewoo You.

COLOR 1

Contrast of value.

Pastels: blue and violet, yellow and orange; gray paper

We will now make a seamless transition from black and white and gray drawing to drawing in color. We begin simply by observing that colors, in addition to their properties as hues, also have properties of value. Some are lighter and some are darker. If we take a traditional color wheel, arranged with complementary colors[10] opposite each other, then we observe that the colors at the bottom, blue and violet, are darker; the colors at the top, orange and yellow are lighter; and the colors on the two sides, red and green, are in the middle.

For this exercise we will take the two complementary colors with the greatest difference in value between them, yellow/orange and blue/violet. Merely substitute them for the roles you gave white and black prismacolor in the previous exercise.

Some of the issues of the previous exercise remain. Look for a subject with a substantial range of value. Try to construe it in a way that serves your intent, and gives the gray space meaning in the exercise. The paper is one of the materials of the exercise.

[10]Complementary colors: Balanced opposites on the color wheel, for example: red and green. For a more detailed discussion, see Color 4 on pg. 140 in this chapter.

Figure 3.40 Derek Rubinoff.

Comments: *I find an easy diagonal stroke (lower left to upper right, if you are right-handed) is a good way to work quickly and at the same time achieve an atmospheric effect. Another approach (shown in Figure 3.44) is to use the page as a lighter value rather than in the middle. In this approach, you work fairly monochromatically using the blue/violet as you used black in the previous exercise.*

Figure 3.41 Derek Rubinoff.

Figure 3.42 Ingrid Moulton Wood.

Figure 3.43 Yellow is the lightest color, blue and blue violet the darkest.

Figure 3.44 Hia Phua.

COLOR 2

Color temperature and color perspective.

Pastels: red and orange, blue and green; gray paper

It is said that "warm" colors tend to advance and that "cool" colors tend to recede. This is not just the musing of interior decorators evaluating the effects of wallpapers. There is a physiological basis for this effect.

As you will remember from Chapter 2 and the discussion of the depth cue *accommodation*, small muscles in the eyes work to slightly change the shape of the lens to focus very near objects onto the retina. The registration of this muscle action is what yields a sense of depth. Thus, we sense the nearness of things through the action of having to accommodate for them.

It turns out that colors are focused at different distances, and that some accommodation is necessary to focus them on the retina. It also turns out that for "warm" colors, colors in the red and orange part of the spectrum, the muscular action of accommodation is similar to the action used to focus near objects. Likewise, the action for "cool" colors, those in the blue and green range, is similar to the action for far objects. This is the basis for what is called *color perspective*, and it is the basis for this exercise.[11]

Find an architectural scene with significant and well-articulated depth. A layered scene with interesting overlaps will serve well. Represent the depth in the scene as an

Figure 3.45 Christopher Ilg.

issue of color temperature. Use red and orange to advance some areas; use blue and green to let other areas recede. Use the gray paper as a neutral condition.

Comments: *Color temperature is used to reverse effect in the drawing in Figure 3.46; that is, to pull forward into our attention an area (the window) that is in the background: a figure-ground reversal of sorts. Color temperature is used for two purpos-*

Figure 3.46 Andrew Kikta.

es in Figure 3.45. It is used both to indicate the color of the light falling on the sculpture, and to advance some areas. The color perspective arises in the intensity with which the warmth of near areas of light is described.

---

[11] Libby, William Charles. *Color and the Structural Sense* (Englewood Cliffs, NJ: Prentice-Hall, Inc., 1974), pp. 67–68.

Figure 3.47 Michael L. Gallin.

Figure 3.48 Cherie Hayek.

COLOR 3

Color temperature and mood of light.

Pastels on gray paper

Light and color can carry different moods. We associate different colors with different seasons, times of day, and their related moods. Light reflecting off a snowy surface is often cooler. Light emanating from a fireplace is warmer.

Our ability to see colors at various times of day also affects the moods we associate with them. Under the low light levels of evening, blue is the color we are still best able to see; the other colors tend to retire. This is the reason why moonlight seems so rendered in blue and why "the blues" are tied to the moods of night and not day.

This exercise is directed at these color differences and the mood effects they produce.

Draw an architectural scene that has a definite mood. A room at sunset, an interior with garish light, or a room receiving light off an exterior surface of newly fallen snow would be good examples.

Comments: *One reason the drawing in Figure 3.47 is so effective in describing light is that it describes only light. It remains vague about surface. Edges and corners remain barely discernible.*

COLOR 4
Complementary contrast.

Pastels: complements on gray charcoal paper

Complementary colors are balanced opposites. When mixed with each other, they cancel each other out. Red mixed with its complement green results in a gray of sorts called a "chromatic gray." Placed next to each other, complements set each other off. Red and green each seem particularly vibrant in the presence of the other. Every redhead knows to wear green and blue sweaters.

Complementary contrast is a powerful effect. Several years ago, I had cataracts removed. After the patch was removed from the first eye, and while my wife was driving me home, I noticed that all the colors—most of all blue and violet—seemed astonishingly vibrant. That night, I remember looking out into the night at the newly fallen snow. The light from the street light looked its usual warm orange, but the shadow cast by the tree was a vibrant blue/violet. What I experienced that evening was complementary contrast at a fever pitch!

For months, I had been viewing the world through the yellow of the cataracts. Acting as a filter, the cataracts had, in effect, cancelled yellow's complement, violet, out of my vision. Now with their removal, I was ultrasensitive to violet, and for several days walked through a world seemingly awash in violet.

Figure 3.49 Andrew Kikta.

This exercise is based on this phenomenon: the effect complements have on each other. It also addresses another issue of color. It is said that complements balance each other. The word "balance" is used in the sense of a teeter-totter. The one with the other results in a playful balance. The one without the other lacks vitality.

Complementary palettes may be composed of simple pairs, for example, blue/violet versus yellow/orange. Or they may split two pairs of complements against one another. The set of drawings by Andrew (Figures 3.49, 3.50) balance orange with its complement blue. The drawing by Ronni in Figure 3.51 uses red and green as one pair and blue and orange as another. A third possibility, one that is interesting for its slightly off-center chromatic grays, is to set a single color off against a pair of colors—one on either side of its true complement.

Figure 3.50 Andrew Kikta.

Figure 3.51 Ronni Fleisher.

Comments: *As Andrew did, a good study to undertake is to draw the same site at different times of day. Effects of daylight and artificial sources on the rendition of material colors are sometimes startling when first recognized.*

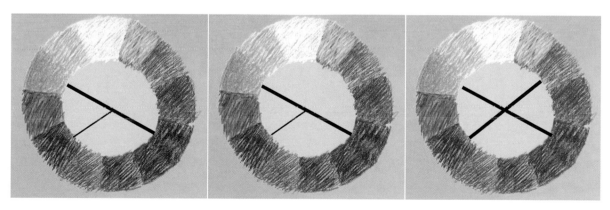

Figure 3.52 In sequence, these are the pallettes used in the images above. In addition, all use yellow and white as tints.

COLOR 5

Color collage.

Color magazine scraps, paste, illustration board

Before trying the extended study with watercolor that will follow this exercise, it is good to gain some confidence in your ability to match one color with another. A great exercise for this purpose is a collage. With a collage made of color scraps, the process is only one of matching. The colors you need already exist. You only have to select those that best apply.

A good scene will have a range of values and hues. There are numerous approaches you can take to this exercise, each one of which has benefits. You can try to match hue, temperature, and value as some of these examples have done. Or you can try to match these issues independently, value but not hue. In their disciplined selectivity, these kinds of approaches often are the most interesting.

Start with a rural scene. Then try a scene that is more architectural.

Comments: *You have to be very patient with color collages. At the outset they progress slowly. They seem to come together at the end and then all at once.*

Figure 3.53 Yvette Kovats.

Figure 3.54 Marc Knowlton.

Figure 3.55 (unknown artist).

Figure 3.56
Robin Kohles.

COLOR 6
A catalogue of appearances.

Watercolors, watercolor paper

Complete a set of watercolors of interiors that focus on windows and play of light.

As with previous drawings, use palettes that emphasize shifts of value. Sometimes, ignore local colors; but when you do match local colors, keep the palette constrained using chromatic grays mixed with two complements. Gradually introduce the issue of temperature (Figure 3.56), but even then keep a very constrained palette.

Figure 3.57 Mark Aufdemberge.

Some Final Thoughts

Figure 3.58 Light and material are paired opposites.

LIGHT AND DARK AND COMPOSITION

The first chapter opened with Nicholaides' suspicions about vision and with an affirmation of touch and movement as the foundation for drawing. Later, we used his understanding of contour to establish a connection between observer and scene. So far in this chapter on light and color, we have discussed the importance of contrast of value for depicting views, but we have not addressed its implication for their composition. As I bring this book to a close, I want to address this subject in a way that returns us to where we began: to Nicholaides and the subject of materiality.

Louis I. Kahn (1901–1974) was an architect known for his command of composition in light and dark. He wrote with great eloquence about the interrelatedness of light and the materiality of architecture. He described light and material as paired opposites:

> All material in nature, the mountains and the streams and the air and we, are made of Light which has been spent, and this crumpled mass called material casts a shadow, and the shadow belongs to Light.[12]

In *Silence and Light,* a book of his writings assembled posthumously, he related sight, as Nicholaides did, to the primacy of touch. But in this next passage Kahn was quite clear about what it is that is the province of vision alone.

I thought then that the first feeling must have been touch. Our whole sense of procreation has to do with touch. From the desire to be beautifully in touch came eyesight. To see was only to touch more accurately. These forces within us are beautiful things that you can still feel even though they come from the most primordial, nonformed kind of existence.

From touch there is a striving to touch, not just touch, and from this developed what could be sight. When sight came, the first moment of sight was the realization of beauty. I don't mean beautiful or very beautiful or extremely beautiful. Just simply beauty itself, which is stronger than any of the adjectives you might add to it. It is a total harmony you feel without knowing, without reservation, without criticism, without choice. It is a feeling of total harmony as if you were meeting your maker, the maker being that of nature, because nature is the maker of all that is made. You cannot design anything without nature helping you.[13]

I close then with two possibilities for using light to compose views. The first is to move toward light, in Kahn's understanding, toward the source. The second is to move toward dark. As archetypes, the former expresses a sense of longing, the latter a sense of mystery.

---

[12] Lobell, John. *Between Silence and Light: Spirit in the Architecture of Louis I. Kahn* (Boulder, CO: Shambhala Publications, Inc., 1979), p. 5.

[13] *Ibid.,* p. 8.

Figures 3.59a and b To move toward light carries a sense of longing; to move toward shadow, a sense of mystery.

Appendices

Figure A.1 David Celento.

Figure A.2 David Celento.

Appendix A

Perspective Projection

HOW TO CONSTRUCT PERSPECTIVE VIEWS

The first method for constructing perspectives using plans and elevations is usually attributed to Piero della Francesca (1420?–1492). It is also possible that Paolo Uccello (1397–1475) might have developed a method as well. Whoever the originator was, the ability to work from orthographic drawings made it possible for the first time to generate views of objects of any shape from any direction. Until that time, Alberti's method of grids had enabled only frontal views and was difficult to use with nonrectangular objects. Over the years, one of the codified methods derived from the early perspectivists came to be called the *office method.* It is this method that is presented here.

We generate perspective views by projecting an image of a subject to or through a picture plane using sight lines. In the office method, we use two separate orthographic views. We use a plan showing the construction from above to enter information about the location of the viewer and the shape and location and orientation of the objects in the

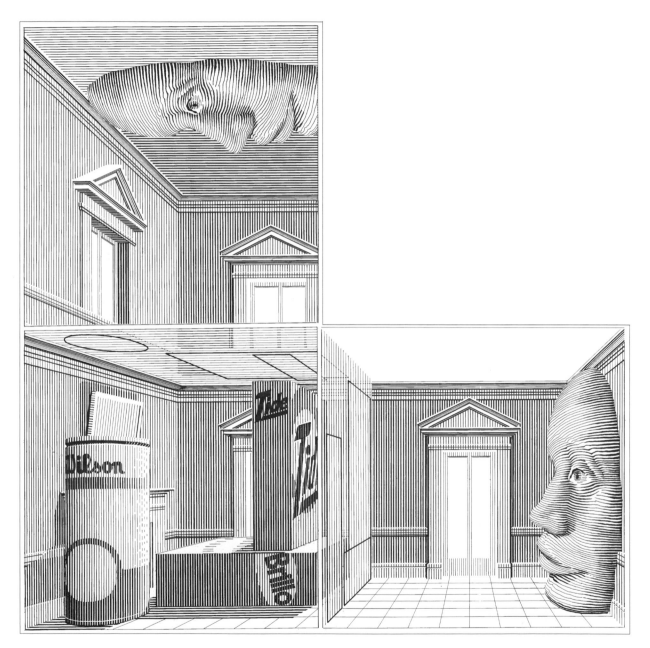

Figure A.3 Perspective uses the views from two directions.

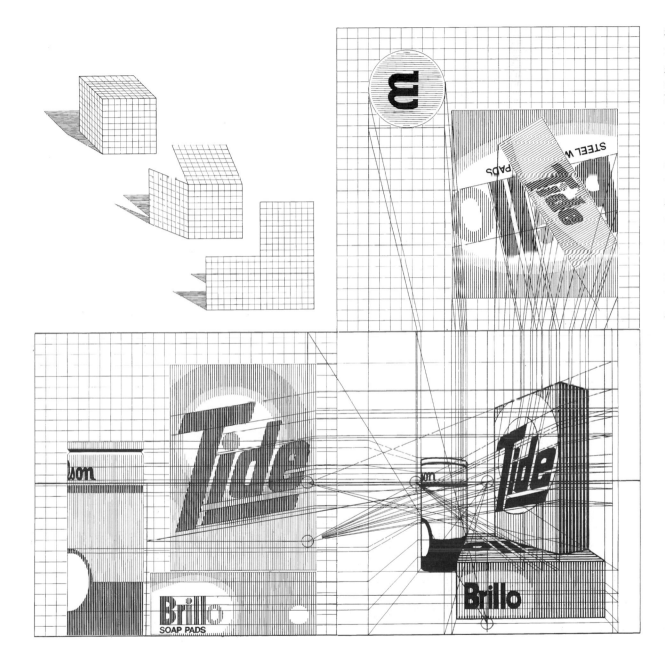

scene. We use an elevation (or section) for information about the height of the viewer's standpoint and the heights of those same objects. We use these two views in combination, bringing them together on the picture plane to form the actual perspective.

Before going any further with the details of the office method, it's best to define some terms. Some of these terms you will understand immediately from the explanation. Others, more complicated, such as the *vertical line of measure*, will take some time to grasp. You will probably need to return to these definitions from time to time as you work through the actual process of generating perspective views.

Figure A.4 The perspective is generated by bringing the two views together into one plane.

The picture plane (PP). The plane where we form the perspective image. It is always perpendicular to the viewer's direction of sight, but we can position it in front of or behind the subject, depending upon the size of the perspective view we desire. If we position the picture plane in front of an object, that object's image will be smaller in the perspective. If we position it behind, the image will be larger.

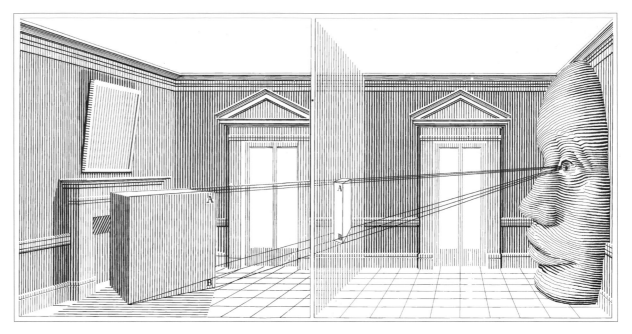

Figure A.5 Picture plane.

Center of vision (CV). The point on the picture plane at which the viewer is looking. In a perspective, the center of vision is always directly opposite (at 90°) the viewer.

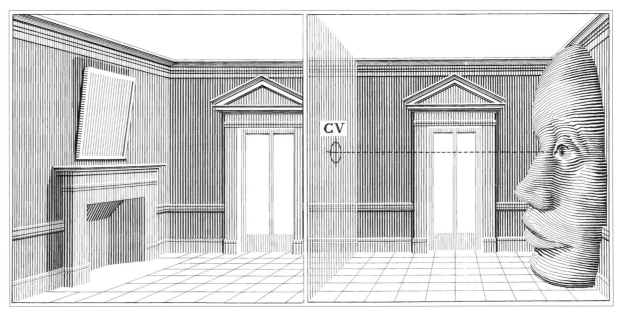

Figure A.6 Center of vision.

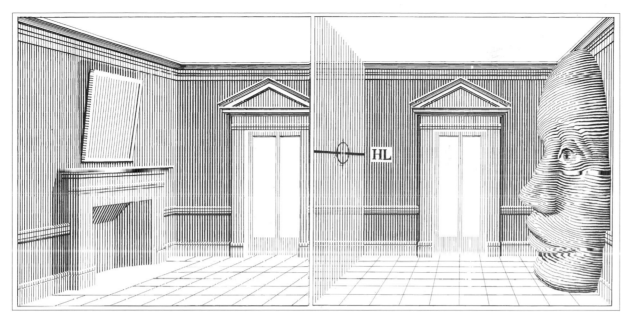

Figure A.7 Horizon line.

Horizon line (HL). The horizon line represents the viewer's height. It is parallel to the ground, and it passes through the center of vision, that point on the picture plane at which the viewer is looking. Vanishing points of all lines that are parallel to the ground are also located along the horizon line. As it is used in perspective practice, the horizon line relates to our use of the word "horizon" in daily life. When we are standing on a beach and looking out horizontally across the water, the ocean does indeed appear to reach a horizon at an infinite distance from us. And just as it is in a perspective construction, that horizon will appear to be located at the same height as our eyes.

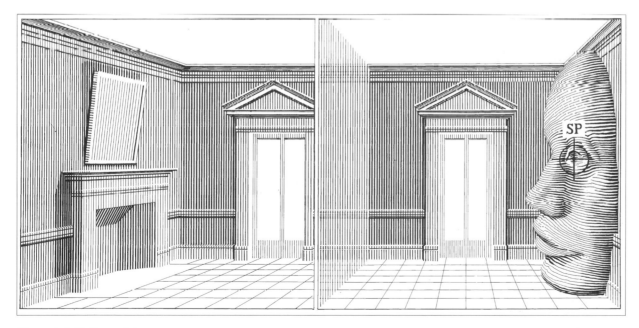

Figure A.8 Station point.

Station point (SP). The position of the viewer as shown in the plan.

Cone of vision. The breadth of field of a perspective view. Owing to the fact that the picture plane only approximates the surface of the retina—it is flat, whereas the retina is curved—the further from the center of vision objects are located the more they will tend to appear distorted. It is generally accepted that to avoid undue distortion, the breadth of field of a perspective view should not exceed 60°. Therefore, early in the process of generating a perspective, we check a view's breadth of field by drawing a 60° cone radiating outward from the viewer's station point in the plan. As long as objects fit within this cone, we can expect they will look okay.

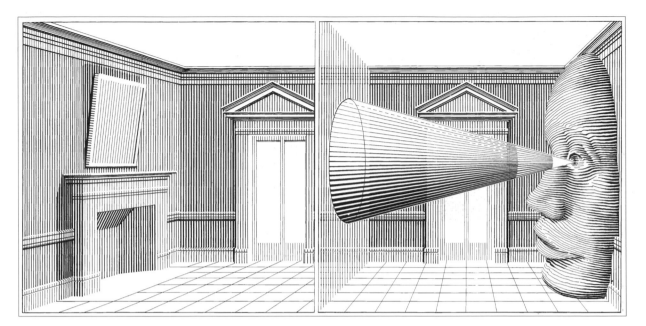

Figure A.9 Cone of vision.

Sight line. We use sight lines to locate points on the picture plane (and in the perspective view) that correspond to points on the objects in the scene. Typically, we draw them in the plan. When an object is in front of the picture plane, we draw sight lines from the station point to the object and extend them back to picture plane. When an object is behind the picture plane, we draw them from the station point through the picture plane to the object behind.

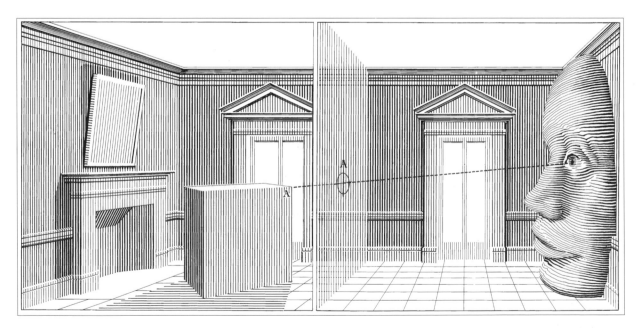

Figure A.10 Sight line.

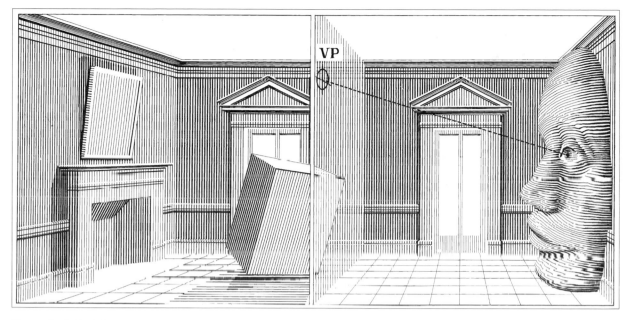

Figure A.11 Vanishing point.

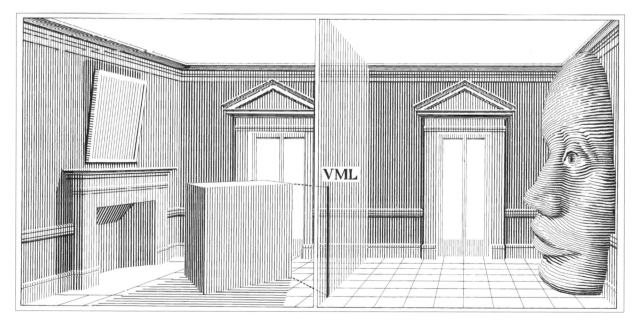

Figure A.12 Vertical measuring line.

Vanishing point (VP). A point on the picture plane at which a set of parallel lines appear to converge. Assuming that the set of parallel lines is level (parallel to the ground: e.g., courses of bricks, windowsills, eaves, and cornices), the vanishing point for that set is found in this way. In the plan, we draw a line parallel to the set from the station point out to a point of intersection with the picture plane. Then we transfer that point of intersection directly to the horizon line. That point on the horizon line serves as the vanishing point for the set of parallel lines.

Vertical measuring line (VML). It is a rule of perspective projection that the picture plane is the only location where things can be measured to scale. The vertical measure line is a scaled vertical line on the picture plane, and we use it to enter information about the heights of objects and their details into the perspective view. When an object already intersects the picture plane, we need not generate a VLM. We can measure heights directly along its existing line of intersection with the picture plane. However, when an object does not intersect the picture plane, we must generate a VLM. This is not difficult to do. We merely extend a plane on the object either forward (as shown in Figure A.12) or back to the picture plane. Then we measure heights along that newly generated line of intersection with the picture plane, the VLM, and with convergent lines transfer these heights to the object itself.

PERSPECTIVE PROJECTION

Office Method

Step 1: Locating the station point. As I stated earlier, perspective is unique among drawing systems in that it yields the view from one individual and singular point in space. We begin the construction process with the location of that unique point called the *station point.*

1.1 Determine the desired direction from which you will view the building (frontal, lateral, etc.). Then position the plan accordingly, with the direction of view represented with a vertical line on your drawing board.

1.2 Decide how much of the building you want to show. Do you want to show the whole building, in which case you would want to stand further away, or do you want to show a detail of the building, in which case you would want to stand closer?

1.3 Locate the station point (SP) along the line representing the direction of view. It should be positioned far enough away from the building so you can fit whatever parts of the building you want to show within a reasonable cone of vision. For most uses, a reasonable cone of vision can be as great as 60°. In the example at right, a more conservative 30° cone of vision has been used.

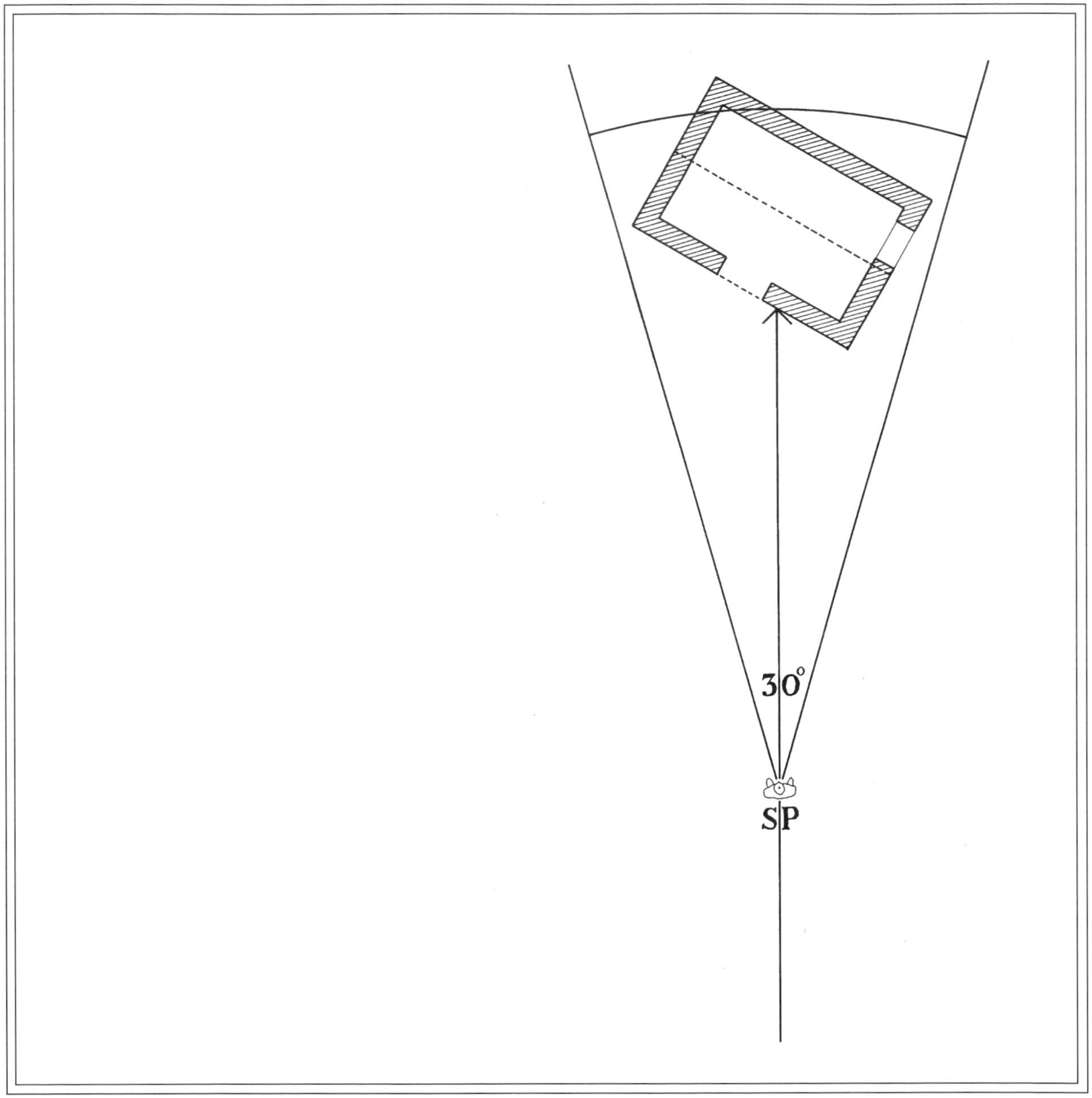

Figure A.13 Office method step 1.

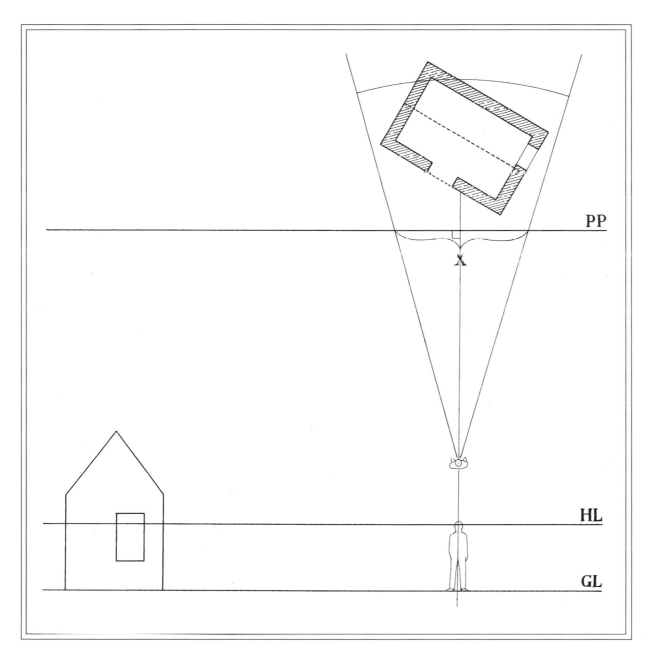

PP

x

HL

GL

Step 2: Locating the picture plane. It is on the picture plane that we construct a perspective. We locate the picture plane in this way:

2.1 First you need to determine the size of the view. You might base this decision on: 1) the size of available paper, 2) the medium to be used and its implications as to size, 3) the level of detail desirable in the view, and 4) the distances from which the drawing is to be viewed.

2.2 Position the picture plane (PP) in the plan so that the picture plane intercepts your cone of vision at a width x equal to your desired width for the view. Remember, the picture plane must be perpendicular to your line of sight.

2.3 Square to the line of sight and to the left (or right) of the area where you will draw the perspective, position an elevation or section of the building. Then, at appropriate heights on that elevation, draw horizontals representing the ground line (GL) and the horizon line (HL). The horizon line represents the height of the viewer's eye. Its height above the ground is drawn to scale: at the same scale as the elevation.

Figure A.14 Office method step 2.

Step 3: Locating vanishing points. It is because of vanishing points that perspectives achieve their sense of depth. Locate vanishing points for sets of horizontal lines with this procedure.

3.1 In plan, draw lines parallel to the sets of lines (side A and side B) for which you want to find vanishing points. These lines should be drawn from the station point (SP) out to points of intersection with the picture plane (PP).

3.2 Transfer these points of intersection with the picture plane (PP) to equivalent positions on the horizon line (HL). These resultant points are the vanishing points for the two sides of the building: vanishing point left (VPL) for side A and vanishing point right (VPR) for side B.

Step 4: Locating the vertical line of measure. While perspectives are not scaled drawings representing true dimensions, we still draw them with reference to the true sizes of objects. In positioning the plan, picture plane, and station point, we have already entered the true widths, depths, and locations of objects into our perspective drawing. But entering their vertical information is somewhat more complicated.

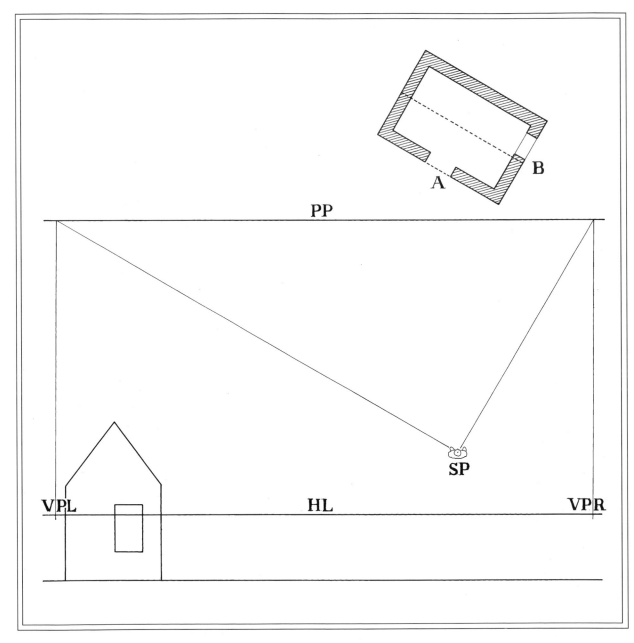

Figure A.15 Office method step 3.

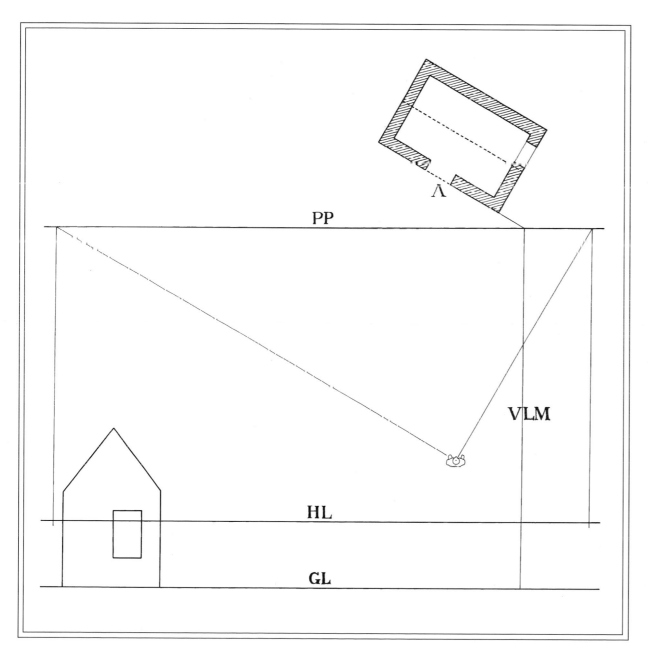

PP

Λ

VLM

HL

GL

We enter it first by generating an auxiliary line called the *vertical line of measure*. Because the picture plane is the only location where we can draw to scale, we must locate this line on the picture plane. Sometimes this is easy. If the object already intersects the picture plane, we need only use that line of intersection directly. However, if the object is behind or in front of the picture plane, we must extend one of its planes until it intersects the picture plane. We develop the vertical information there, then transfer it to the object using the appropriate vanishing points. Since the house in our view does not already intersect the picture plane, we have to extend one of its planes forward.

4.1 In plan, extend side A to a point of intersection with the picture plane (PP). (If side A had already intersected the picture plane, you could have proceeded directly to step 4.2.)

4.2 Project that point of intersection vertically down the drawing until it crosses both the horizon line (HL) and the ground line (GL). This vertical line is the vertical line of measure (VLM). (If side A had already intersected the picture plane, you would have merely projected the VLM from that point of intersection.)

Figure A.16 Office method step 4.

Step 5: Entering vertical information.
Usually, we enter vertical information by using a preexisting section or elevation, such as the one already positioned in the drawing in Figure A.17. The process is one of merely projecting that information over to the vertical line of measure (VLM).

5.1 From relevant points on the elevation of side A or side B, project horizontals to points of intersection with the vertical line of measure (VLM).

5.2 From these points of intersection, converge this vertical information to the vanishing point of side A (VPL).

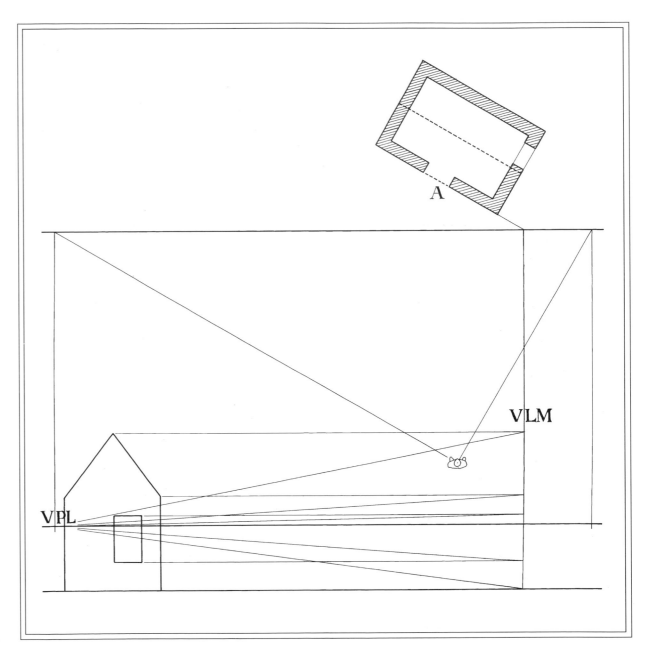

Figure A.17 Office method step 5.

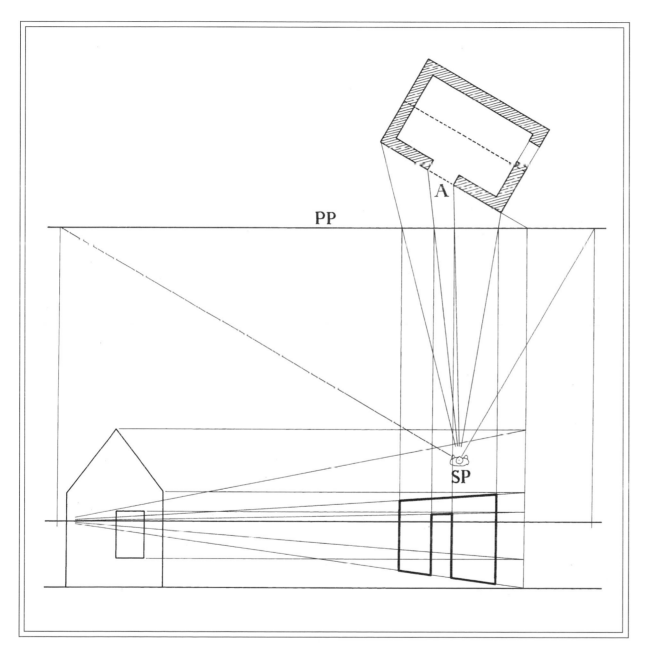

Step 6: Constructing one face. You now have sufficient vertical information to construct the perspective of the building. Begin by representing one face of the building. Then use this part to generate the rest. Side A can serve this purpose. Because you have already generated the information about its heights (step 5.2), you can immediately begin to sight its lateral information: its two ends and the location of the door.

6.1 In plan, sight relevant points along side A to points of intersection with the picture plane. Draw sight lines from the station point back through the picture plane to points on the wall. Where these sight lines cross the picture plane, draw vertical lines.

6.2 Use these vertical lines in concert with the convergent lines on side A to complete the perspective view of side A.

Figure A.18 Office method step 6.

Step 7: Completing the perspective. From the roof peak, base and edges of side A, converge lines to VPR.

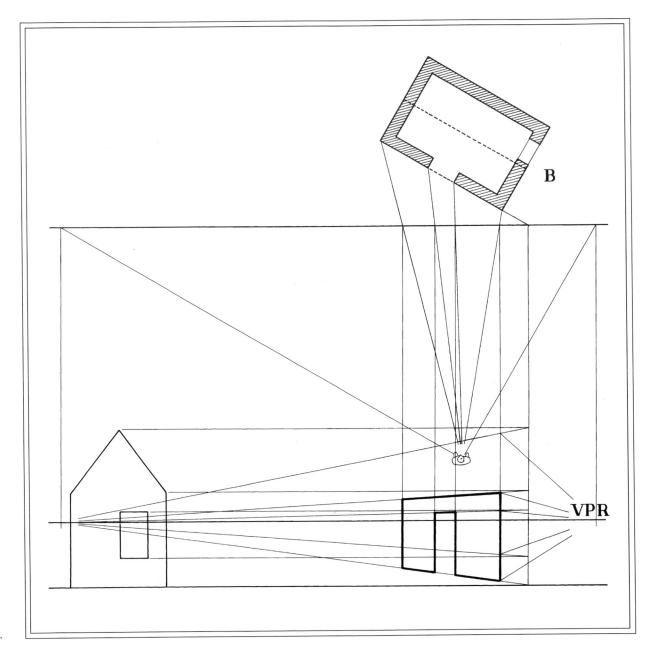

Figure A.19 Office method step 7.

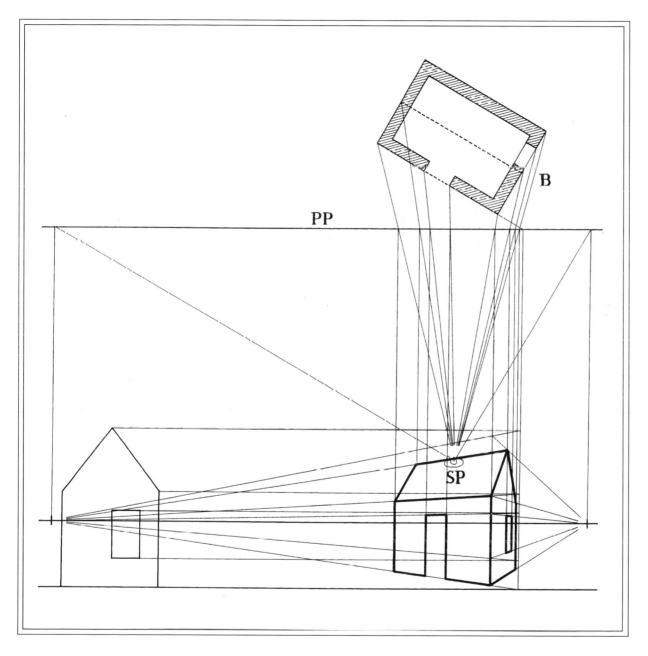

Step 8: Completing the perspective. Construct side B and the roof planes. In plan, sight relevant points along side B to points of intersection with the picture plane. Draw sight lines from the station point back through the picture plane to points on the house. Where these sight lines cross the picture plane, project lines directly to the perspective view and flesh out the view accordingly.

PP

B

SP

Figure A.20 Office method step 8.

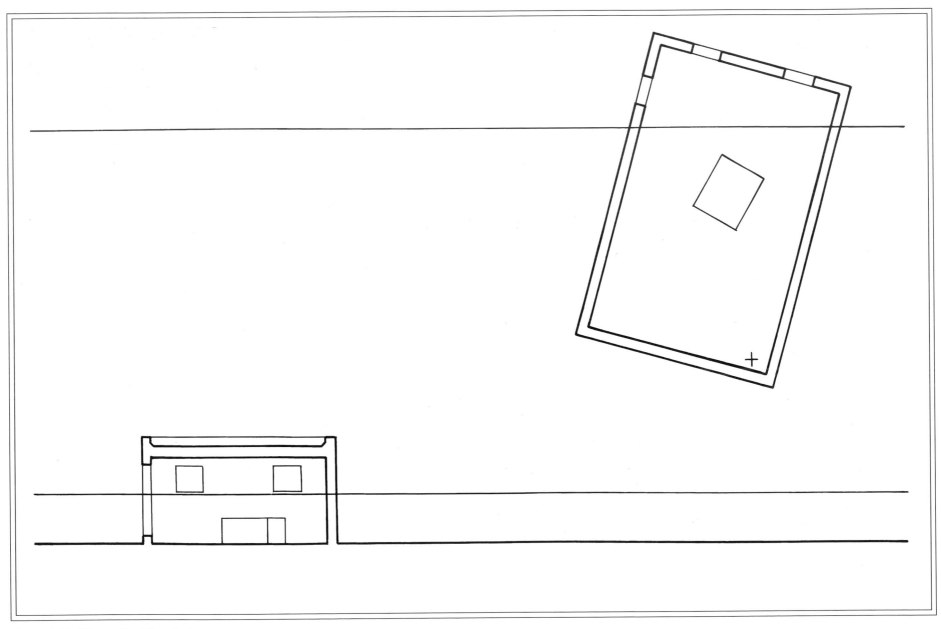

Figure A.21 Office method, Exercise 1.

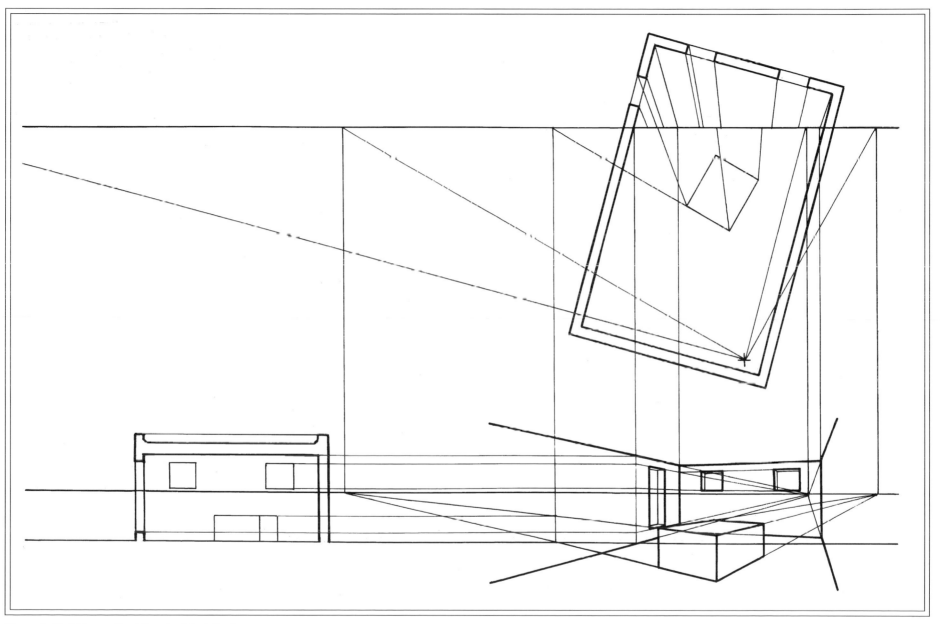

Figure A.22 Office method, Exercise 1 (solution).

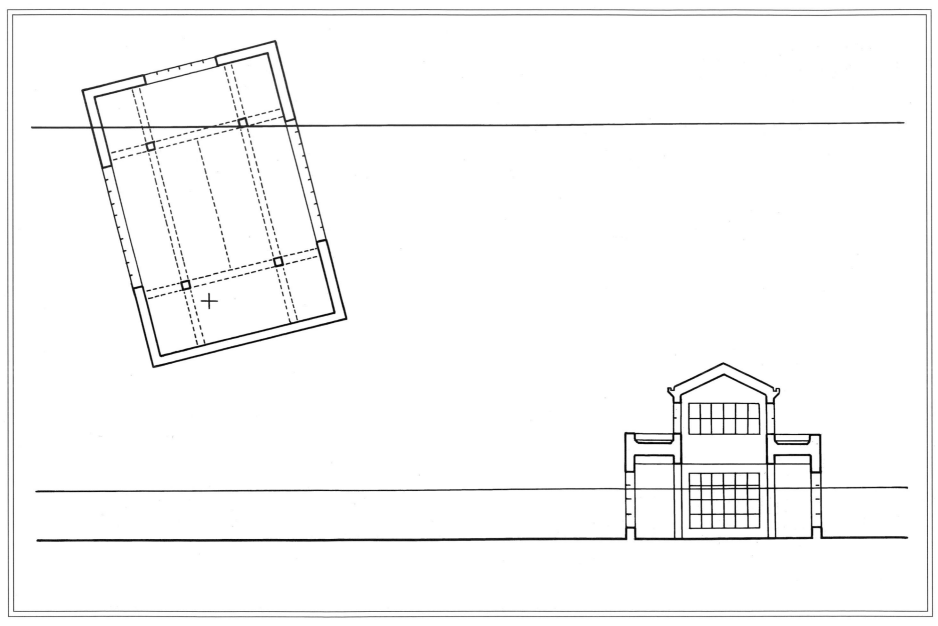

Figure A.23 Office method, Exercise 2.

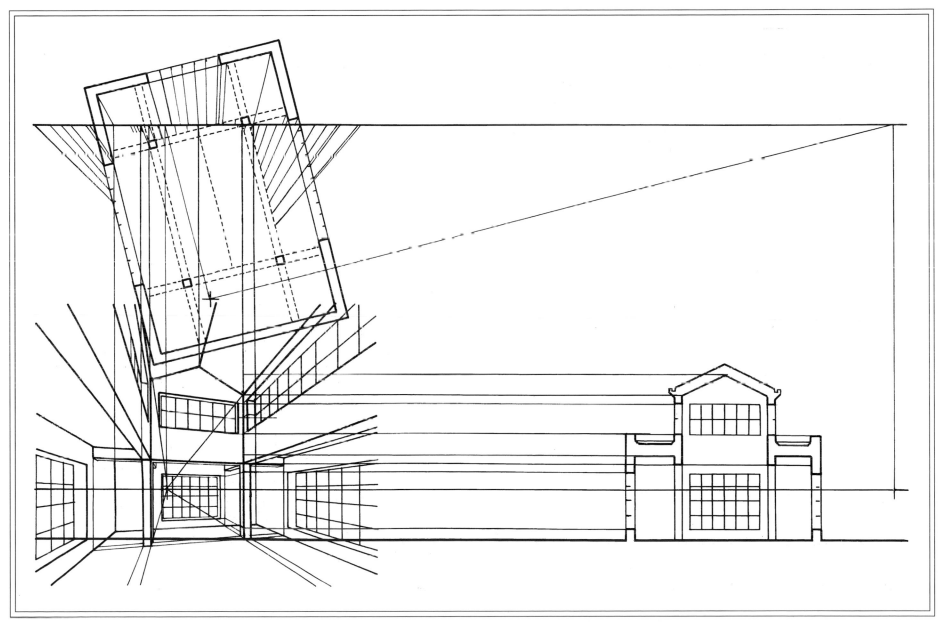

Figure A.24 Office method, Exercise 2 (solution).

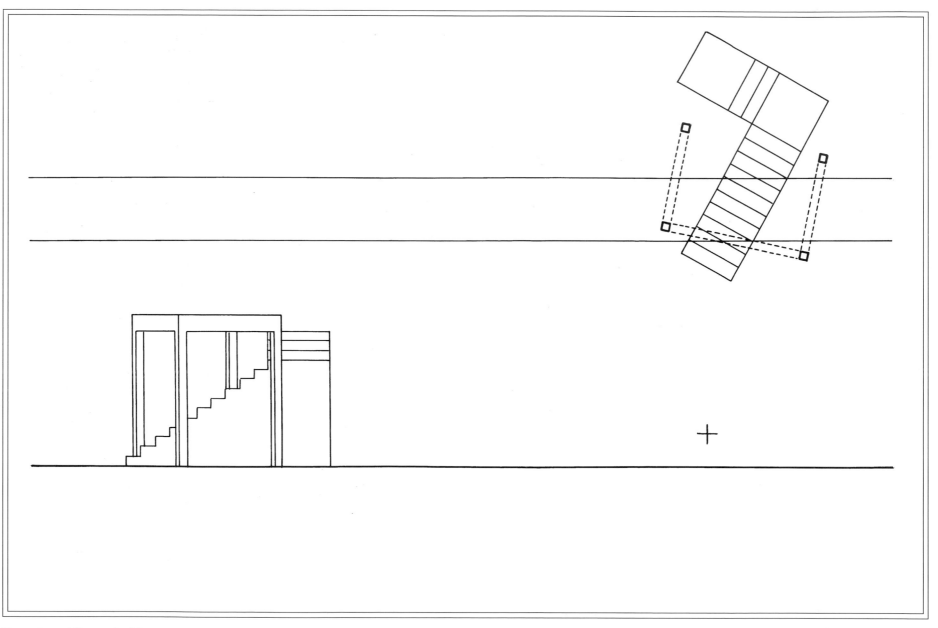

Figure A.25 Office method, Exercise 3.

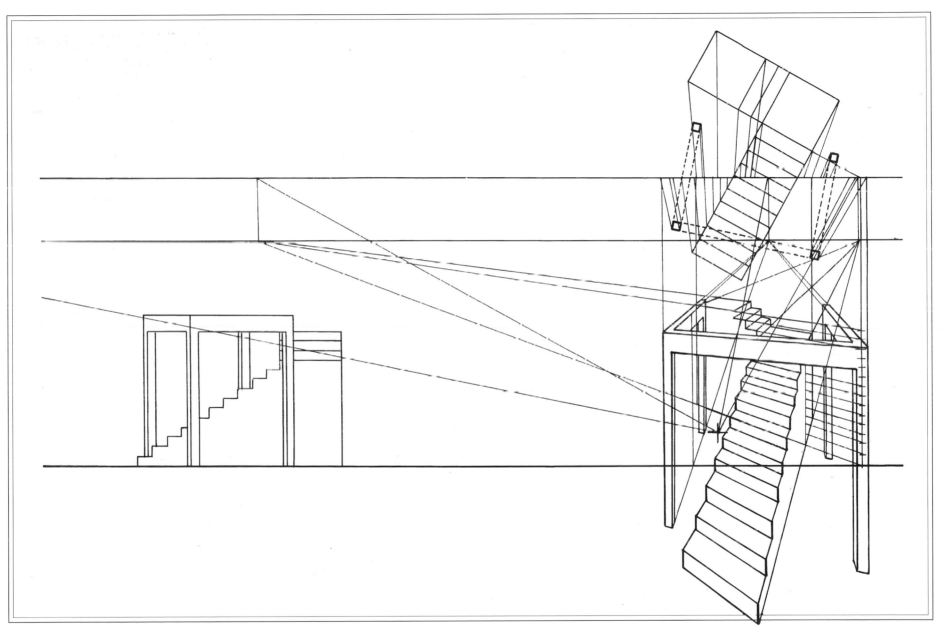

Figure A.26 Office method, Exercise 3 (solution).

One-Point Magic Method

Using a one-point view construction called the *magic method,* we can dispense altogether with the process of sighting on plans and generating vertical lines of measure. In their place, we represent foreshortening and location using Alberti's system, the *Construzione Leggitima,* from the mid-fifteenth century. That method, using distance points on a section or elevation, had concluded a long search for an accurate method to determine foreshortening. Though limited effectively to one-point perspective views, the magic method is enormously useful because it is so simple. Because of their speed, magic views are used to rapidly test design proposals at an early point in the design process.

The magic method is based on the fact that the vanishing point of a 45° spatial diagonal must be the same distance, to the left or right of the central vanishing point, as the viewer is standing from the picture plane. This owes to the fact that 45° triangles have sides of equal length. We are able to locate this point, the vanishing point for a 45° line, without using a station point or projecting lines to the picture plane. We simply lay it out directly on the picture plane (for which an existing section or elevation is conveniently used) by measuring over to the left or right of the central vanishing point the distance of the viewer from the picture plane. We use this vanishing point for a 45° line to measure distances in back of or in front of the picture plane.

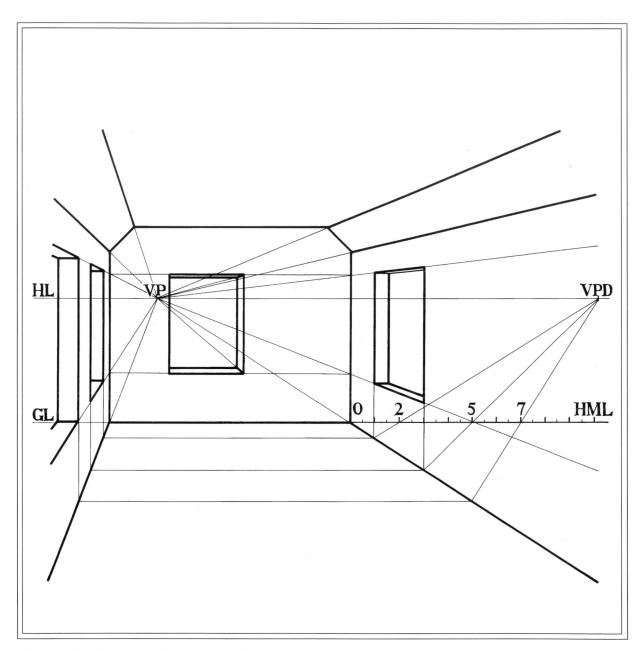

Figure A.27 Magic method using an end-wall elevation.

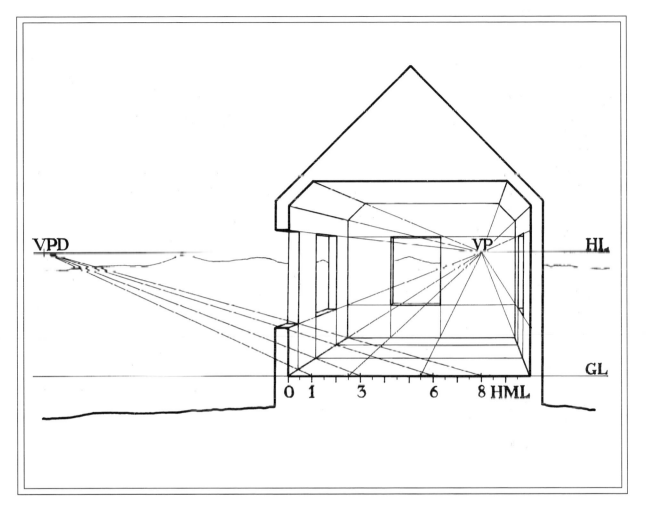

Figure A.28 Magic method using a section.

There are two types of magic views. One uses an end-wall elevation for its picture plane, the other a cross-section. The former develops the view out from the end-wall; the latter behind the section.

Interior from an elevation

1. Draw ground and horizon lines (GL, HL).
2. Locate central vanishing point (VP).
3. Locate vanishing point for diagonal (VPD) left or right of central vanishing point.
4. Use VP to vanish edges of floor, ceiling, and other relevant points out from the elevation.
5. Construct a horizontal measuring line (HML) located along the ground line so that zero (no depth from the elevation) is at the lower left or right outside corner of the elevation.
6. Use HML together with VPD to project increments of depth to the right or left edge of the floor, and project these points out into the interior of the room. See Figure A.27.

Interior from a section

1. Draw ground and horizon lines (GL, HL).
2. Locate the central vanishing point (VP).
3. Locate the vanishing point for the diagonal (VPD) left or right of the central vanishing point.
4. Vanish edges of ceilings, floors, walls, and other relevant points from the section back toward the VP.
6. Construct a horizontal measuring line (HML). HML should be located along the ground line so that zero (no depth from the section) is at the lower-left or right-inside corner of the section. Use HML together with VPD to project increments of depth to the right or left edge of floor, and project these points out into the interior of the room. See Figure A.28.[1]

---

[1] Kevin Forseth, *Graphics for Architecture* (New York: Van Nostrand Reinhold Co., 1980), p. 140–142.

Figure A.29 Andrew Kitka.

Figure A.30 Andrew Kitka.

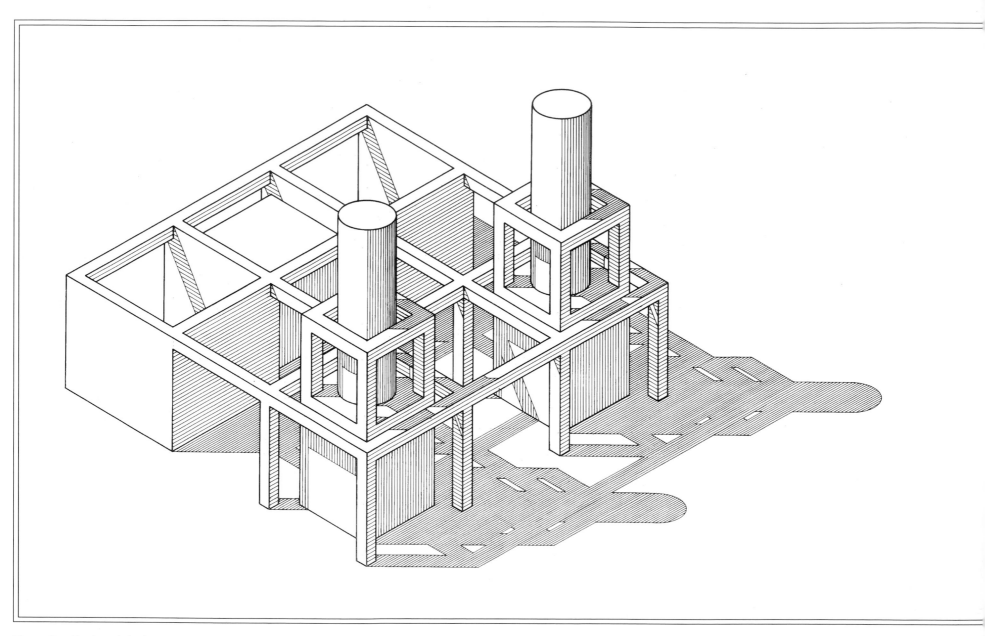

Figure B.1 Shade and shadow in isometric projection.

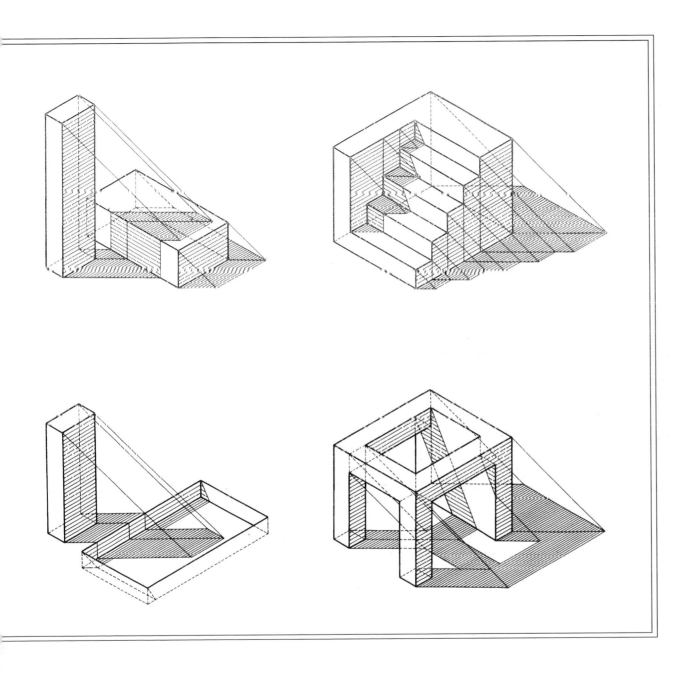

Appendix B

Shade and Shadow in Isometric Projection

This volume concludes with the study of shade and shadow casting in isometric projection and, in the next Appendix, in orthographic projection. In the past, shadow casting always was included in courses on projective geometry, but with the arrival of the computer, it is no longer necessary to construct shadows by hand, and the subject is rarely taught. This is unfortunate because shadow casting was never just a tool. Its significance was (and remains) as a hurdle to teach and test capabilities of three-dimensional visualization.

Because shadow casting is easier to visualize with all three spatial axes visible, we begin it with isometric projection.[1]

---

[1] Adapted from Maxwell G. Mayo, *Line and Light* (Pittsburgh: Department of Architecture, Carnegie Mellon University, 1971), Chapters 1–9.

CONSTRUCTING SHADE AND SHADOW IN ISOMETRIC PROJECTION

Three conventions are used to represent the angle of the light used to project shadows in isometric projection. These conventions are largely a matter of their convenience in using the 30°–60°–90° and 45°–45°–90° triangles that are common to offices. Only one, R°, has any significance beyond convenience, that being that it represents the volumetric diagonal of a cube.

R° light. R° light is represented by a line drawn at an angle of 30° to the horizontal. It is defined as light whose azimuth, measured clockwise from north, is 225°, and whose altitude, measured from the horizontal ground plane, is 35°15'51". R° light falls parallel to the southwest diagonal of a cube oriented normally to the north-south-east-west axes.

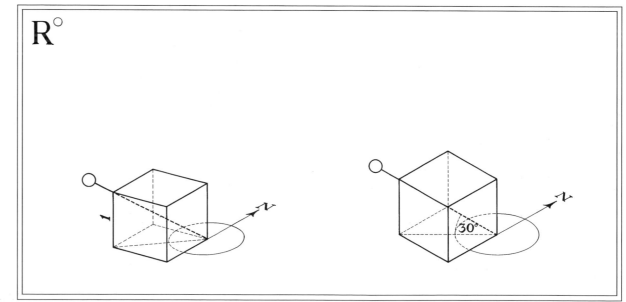

Figure B.2 R° light.

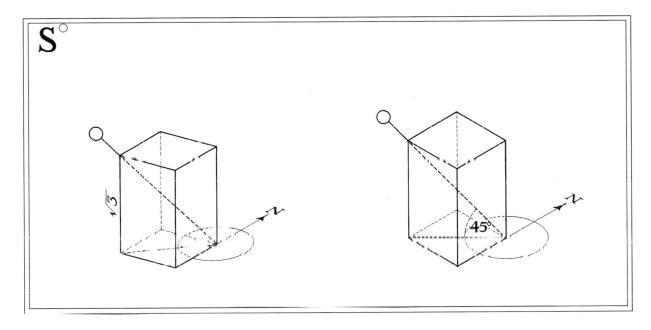
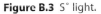

S° light. S° light is represented by a line drawn at an angle of 45° to the horizontal. It is defined as light whose azimuth, measured clockwise from north is 225°, and whose altitude, measured from the horizontal ground plane, is 50°46'15". S° light falls parallel to the southwest diagonal of a $1 \times 1 \times 2$ rectangular solid oriented normally to the north-south-east-west axes.

Figure B.3 S° light.

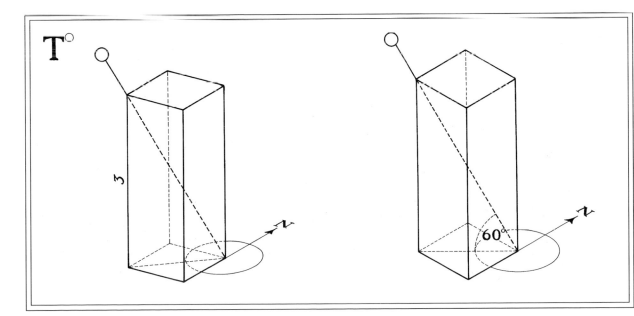
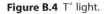

T° light. T° light is represented by a line drawn at an angle of 60° to the horizontal. It is defined as light whose azimuth, measured clockwise from north is 225°, and whose altitude, measured from the horizontal ground line, is 65°45'36". T° light falls parallel to the southwest diagonal of a $1 \times 1 \times 3$ rectangular solid oriented normally to the north-south-east-west axes.

Figure B.4 T° light.

CONSTRUCTING SHADE AND SHADOW IN ISOMETRIC PROJECTION

Casting the shadow of a point using the slicing method. To cast the shadow of a point, pass a vertical plane in the direction of the sun's rays through the object and ground receiving the shadow. The line of intersection this plane makes with the object and the ground is called the *slice line*. The shadow of the point must lie somewhere along this line. Project a ray of the sun through the point and extend it until it intersects the slice. This point of intersection between the ray and slice line is the shadow of the point.

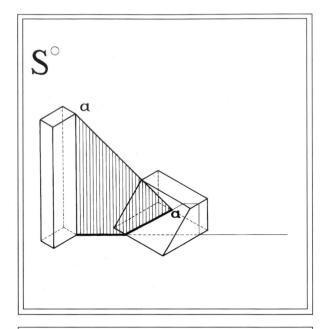

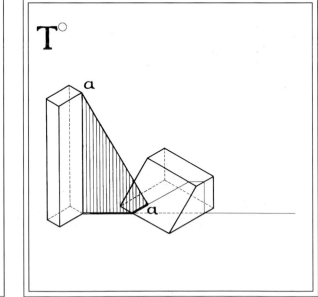

Figure B.5 Casting the shadow of a point.

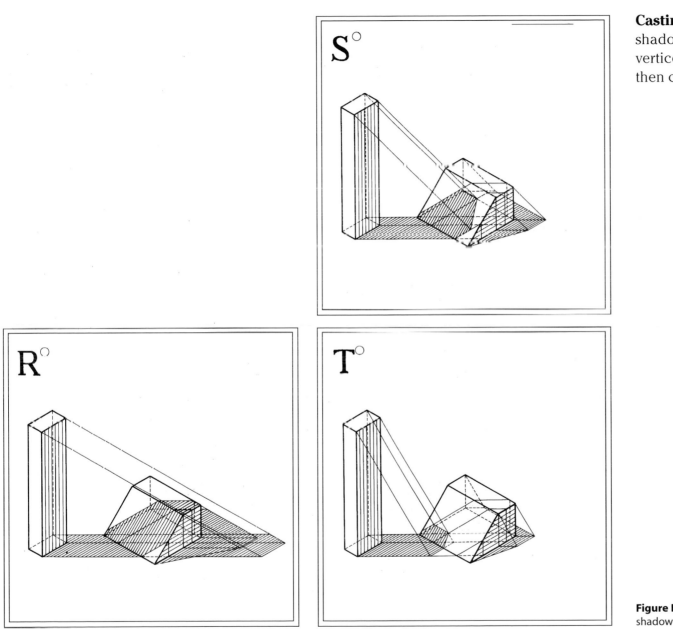

Casting the shadow of a solid. To cast the shadow of a solid, the shadows of the solid's vertices are found via the slicing method and then connected.

Figure B.6 Casting the shadow of a solid.

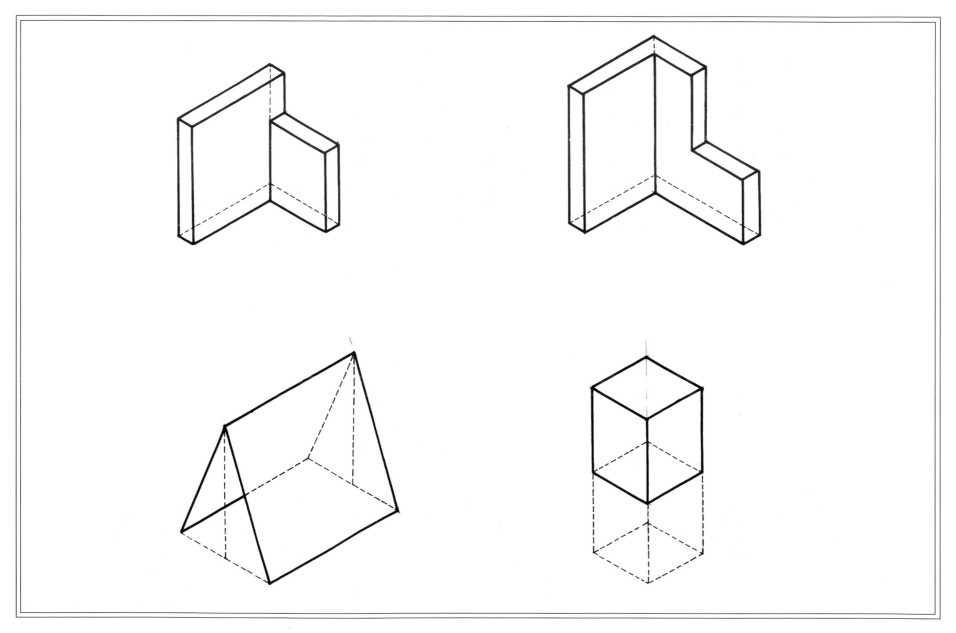

Figure B.7 Shade and shadow in isometric projection, Exercises 1.

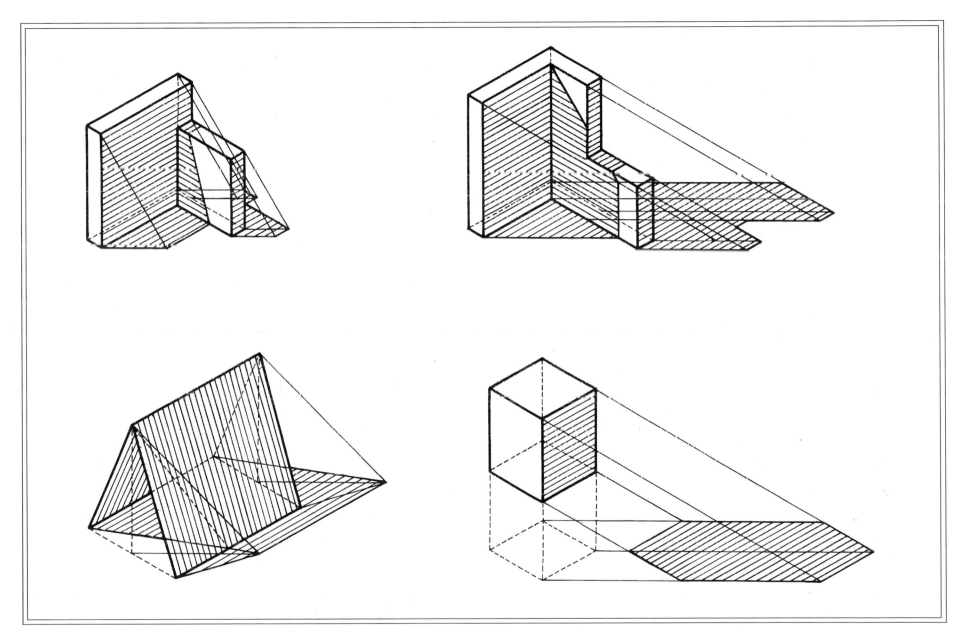

Figure B.8 Shade and shadow in isometric projection, Exercises 1 (solutions).

Figure B.9 Shade and shadow in isometric projection, Exercises 2.

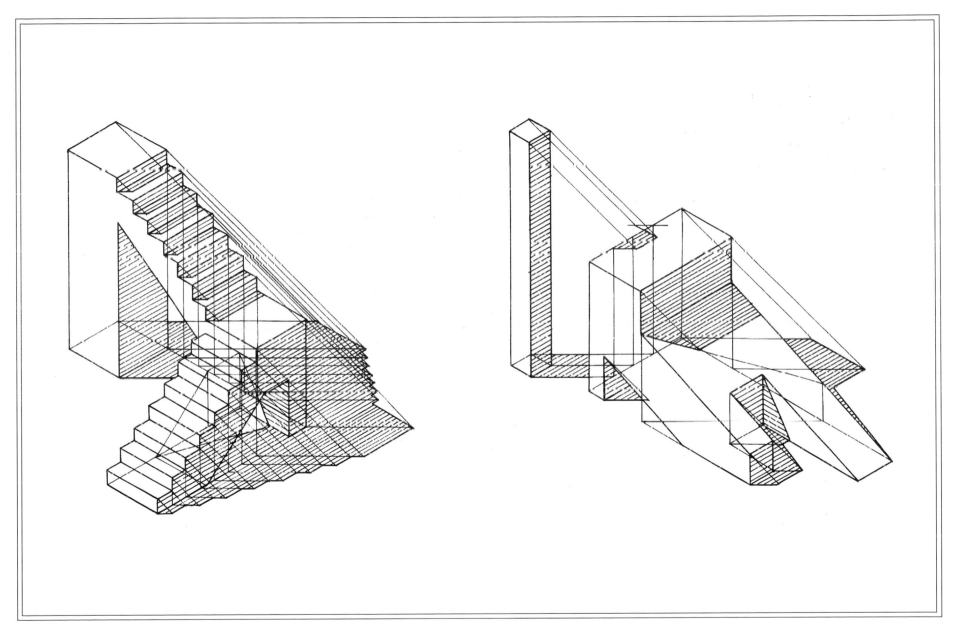

Figure B.10 Shade and shadow in isometric projection, Exercises 2 (solutions).

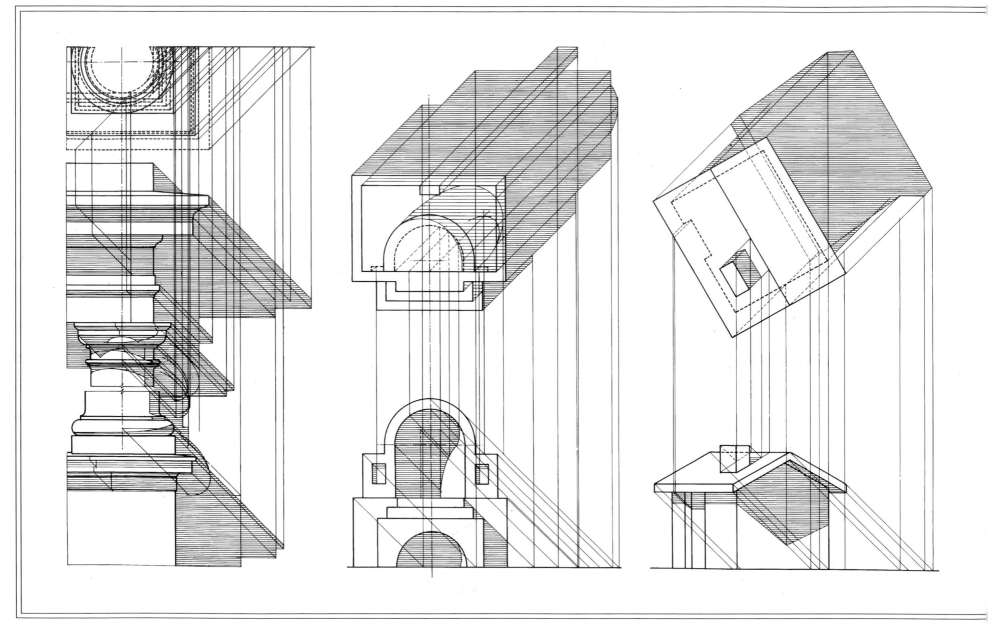

Figure C.1 Shade and shadow in orthographic projection.

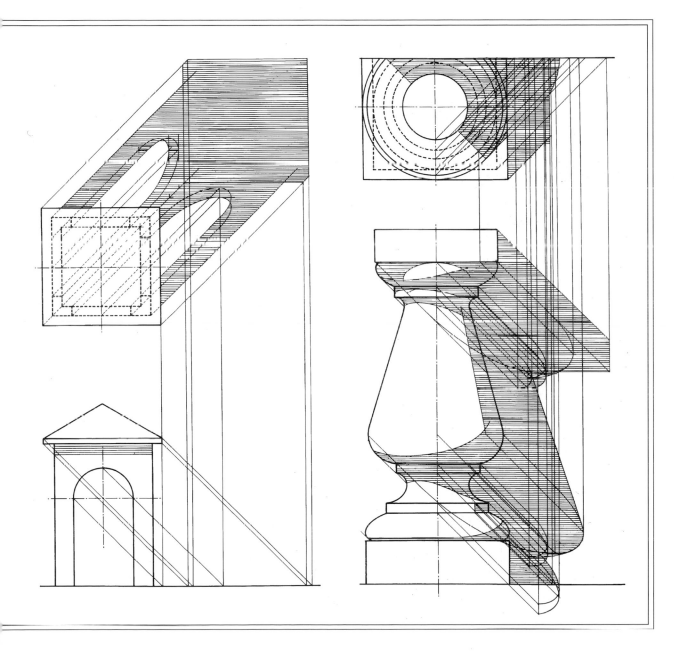

Appendix C

Shade and Shadow in Orthographic Projection

Fundamentally, the process of casting shade and shadow in orthographic projection is the same as it is in isometric projection. Once again, we use a slice line. Likewise, we continue to generate shadows point by point and find the shadow of each point at the intersection of the slice line with the ray.

What is different is that we do the construction over a set of drawings, usually a plan and an elevation, and we refer the process back and forth between them. Even in this there is a regular pattern. It almost always happens that we begin work in the plan, proceed to the elevation, and then conclude work in the plan.[1]

[1] Adapted from Maxwell G. Mayo, *Line and Light* (Pittsburgh: Department of Architecture, Carnegie Mellon University, 1971), Chapters 1–9.

CONSTRUCTING SHADE AND SHADOW IN ORTHOGRAPHIC PROJECTION

There is one convention governing the direction of light in orthographic projection.

R° light. R° light is standard in orthographic projection. When drawn in plan with north oriented vertically, R° light is represented by a line slanting at 45° toward the upper right. When drawn in east and south elevations, R° light is represented by a line slanting at 45° towards the lower right. R° light is the spatial diagonal of a cube. It has an azimuth of 225° from north and an altitude of 35°15'51".

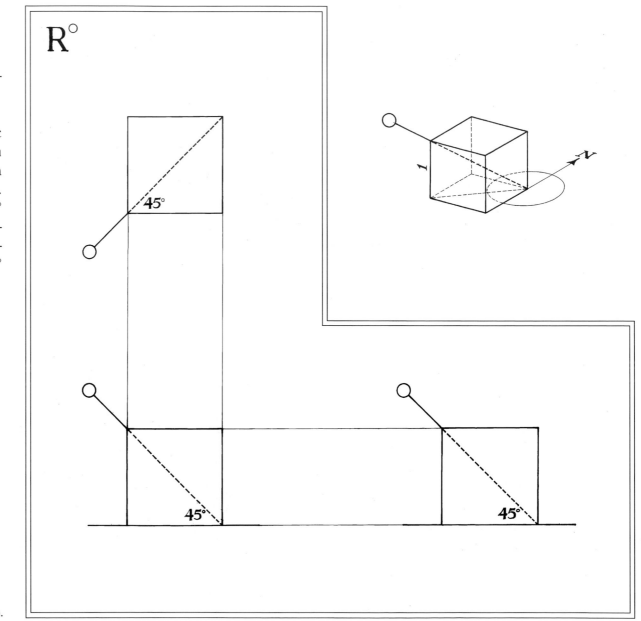

Figure C.2 R° light in orthographic projection.

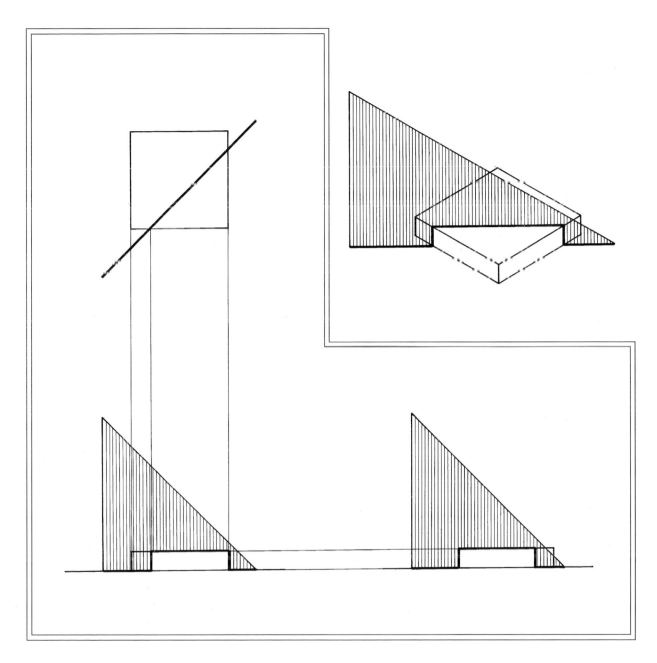

The slicing method. Although the process of casting shadows in orthographic projection is essentially the same as it is in isometric projection, the two differ somewhat in technique. While both use the slicing method, the process in orthographic projection requires using a minimum of two drawings (usually a plan and an elevation) and transferring information from one drawing to another. As part of this two drawing process, the slice is represented in both plan and elevation. Several rules of thumb: 1) In plan, the slice is always represented by a straight line. 2) In elevation, the slice is always represented by a plane.

Figure C.3 The slicing method in orthographic projection.

CONSTRUCTING SHADE AND SHADOW IN ORTHOGRAPHIC PROJECTION

Casting the shadow of a point. To cast the shadow of a point in orthographic projection, pass a vertical plane through the point and the object receiving the shadow. Draw this plane first in plan. Conveniently, it will always be represented with a straight line at 45°. The shadow of the point must lie somewhere along this plan of the slice. Next, through a process of transferring relevant points from the plan of the slice to corresponding points on the objects in the elevation, develop an elevation view of the slice line. The shadow of the point must lie somewhere along this elevation of the slice. Then, in the elevation cast a ray of sunlight through the point and extend it to a point of intersection with the elevation of the slice. This point of intersection is the shadow of the point in elevation. Finally, with a vertical line, transfer this point from the elevation to the plan of the slice in the plan view. This point of intersection is the shadow of the point in plan.

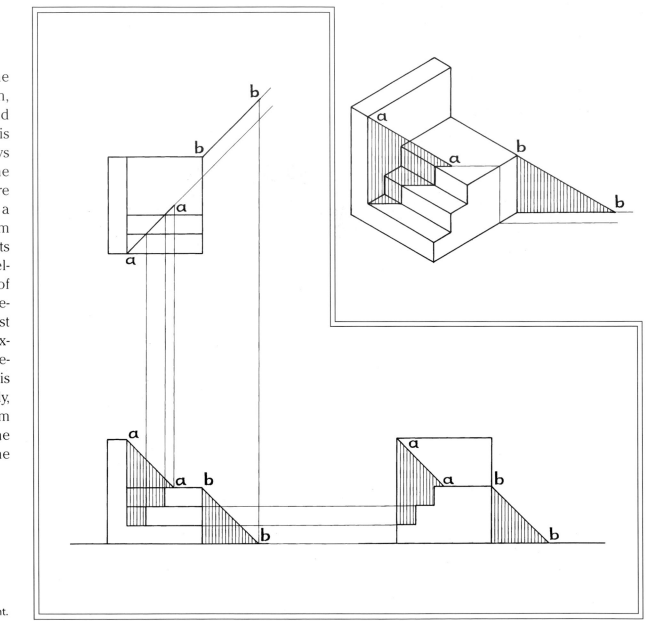

Figure C.4 Casting the shadow of a point.

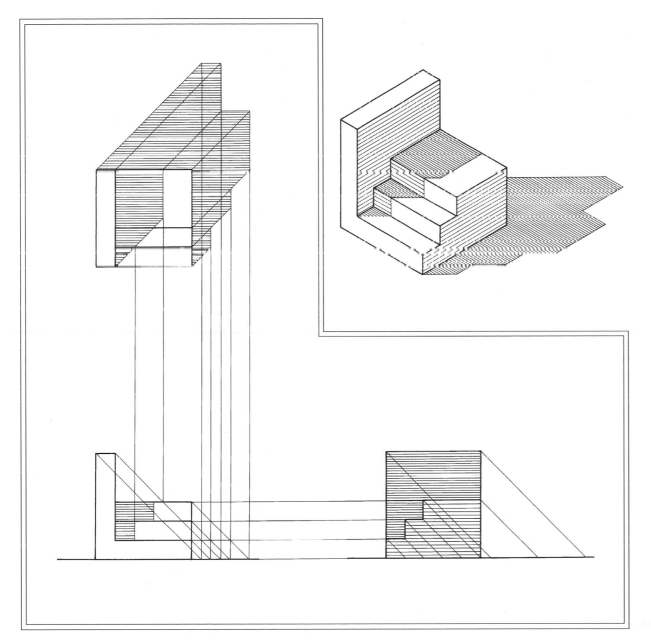

Casting the shadow of a solid. To cast the shadow of a solid, the shadows of the solid's several vertices are found via the slicing method and then connected.

Figure C.5 Casting the shadow of a solid.

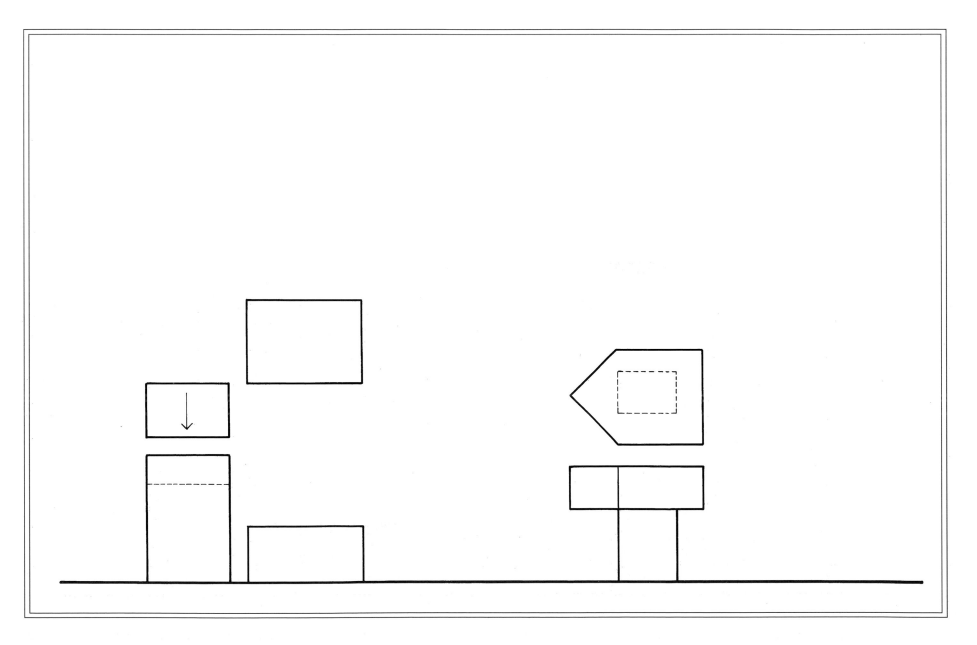

Figure C.6 Shade and shadow in orthographic projection, Exercises 1.

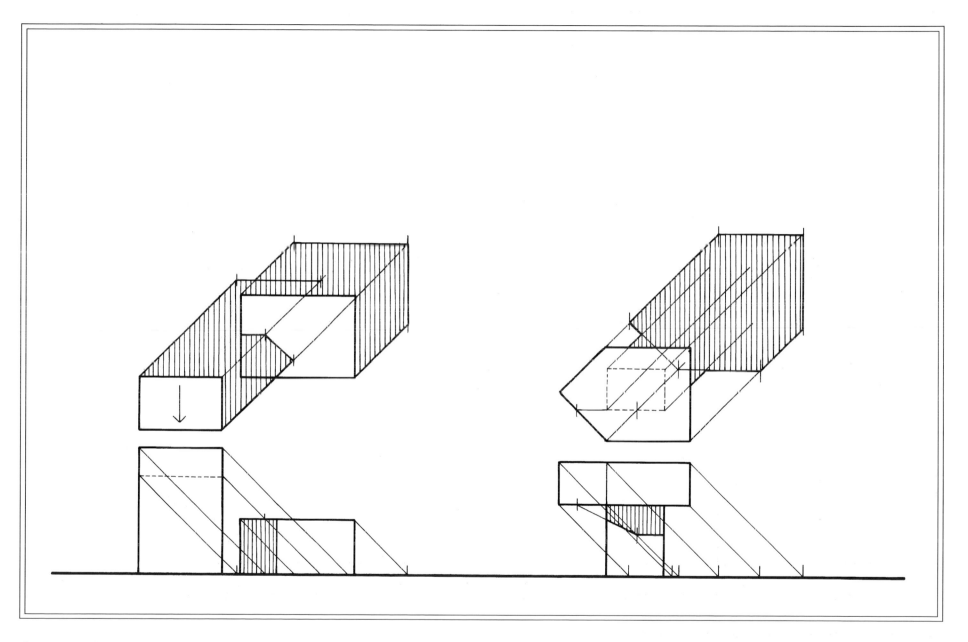

Figure C.7 Shade and shadow in orthographic projection, Exercises 1 (solutions).

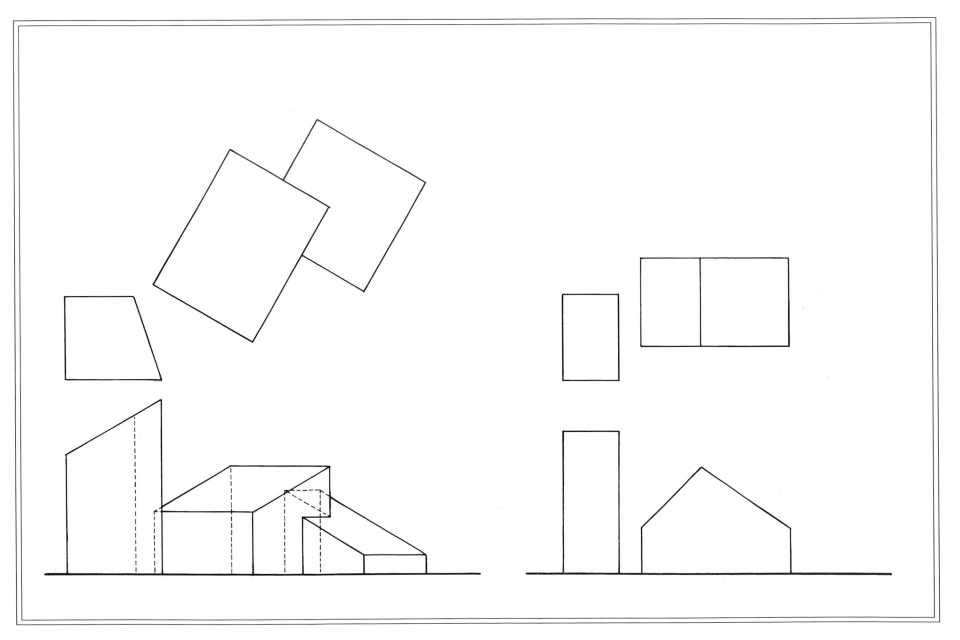

Figure C.8 Shade and shadow in orthographic projection, Exercises 2.

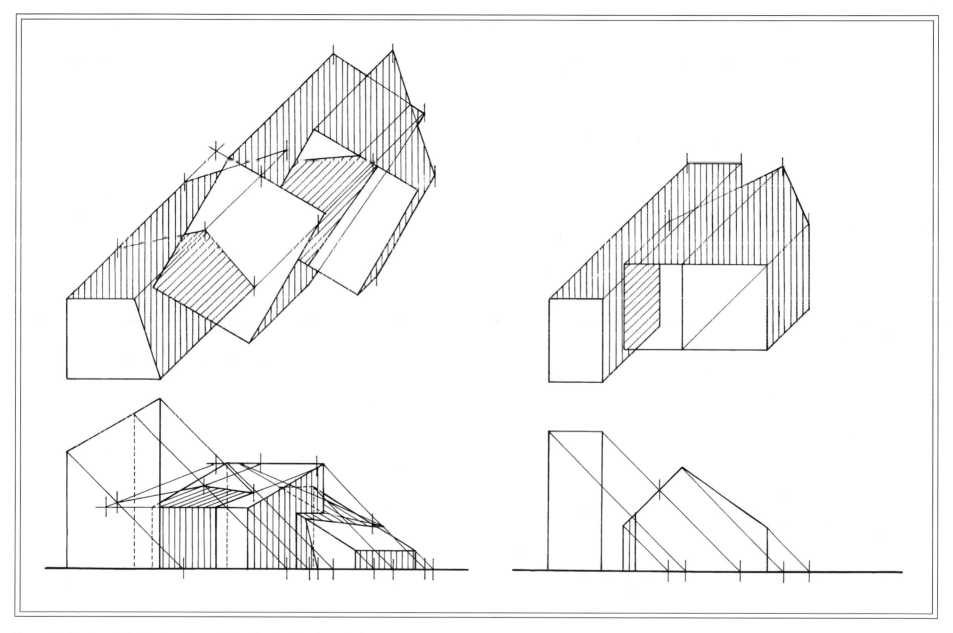

Figure C.9 Shade and shadow in orthographic projection, Exercises 2 (solutions).

Bibliography

Allport, Floyd H. *Theories of Perception and the Concept of Structure*. New York: John Wiley & Sons, 1955. Provides an overview of the process of perceiving, as well as in-depth discussion of various points of view, including Gestalt psychology and transactional psychology.

Arnheim, R. *Art and Visual Perception: A Psychology of the Creative Eye*. New version, expanded and rev. ed. Berkley: University of California Press, 1974. Arnheim's central work considers the perception and representation of shape, form, and space from the perspective of Gestalt psychology. Includes analysis of the development of drawings by children.

Arnheim, R. *Visual Thinking*. Berkley and Los Angeles: University of California Press, 1969. More wide-ranging in its scope than *Art and Visual Perception*. Considers visual perception as a cognitive activity that is both separate from and related to other modes of thought.

Arnheim, R. "Gestalt Psychology and Artistic Form," in *Aspects of Form*. Edited by L. L. Whyte. Bloomington: Indiana University Press, 1966, pp. 196–208.

Barnett, H. G. *Innovation: the Basis of Cultural Change*. New York: McGraw Hill, 1953. Account of the dynamics of perception during the process of design from the general perspective of Gestalt psychology. Appendix, "On Things," provides an excellent account of the perception of qualities of things.

Blanshard, Francis Bradshaw. *Retreat from Likeness in the Theory of Painting*. New York: Columbia University Press, 1949. Provides a brief account from several points of view of the role of appearance in making pictorial art. Includes summaries of the positions of Plato, Aristotle, Reynolds, Plotinus, and Shopenhauer.

Boring, E. G. *Sensation and Perception in the History of Experimental Psychology*. New York: Appleton, 1942. Provides an historical account of changing understandings of perception and changing interpretations of specific phenomena, including the primary and secondary depth cues.

Cooper, D. "Drawings as Substitute Places" in *Dichotomy*. Edited by G. Dodds. Detroit: University of Detroit School of Architecture, 1983, pp. 76–83.

Deregowski, J. B. "Pictorial Perception and Culture," in *Readings from Scientific American*. Edited by R. Held. San Francisco: W. H. Freeman, 1971, pp. 79–85. Based on studies of Zulu tribesmen, presents evidence that visual perception and specifically linear perspective are culturally based.

Dewey, John. *Art as Experience*. A view of art presented by one of the central figures within the transactionalist point of view.

Edgarton, S. Y. *The Renaissance Rediscovery of Linear Perspective*. New York: Basic Books, 1975. Provocative and wide-ranging book that relates the rediscovery of linear perspective at the onset of the 1400s to developments in other fields, including the arrival in Florence of a copy of Ptolemy's *World Atlas*, Columbus' voyage to America, and an overall changing world view. Book includes a detailed account of Brunelleschi's perspective experiments conducted in front of the Baptistery in Florence.

Edwards, Betty. *Drawing on the Right Side of the Brain*. New York: St. Martin's Press, 1979. Presents a drawing pedagogy based on the model put forth by R. W. Sperry, which proposed that spatial reasoning is a function of the right hemisphere of the brain and that verbal reasoning is a function of the left.

Forseth, Kevin. *Graphics for Architecture*. New York: Van Nostrand Reinhold, 1980.

Gardner, Howard. *Art Mind and Body*. New York: Basic Books, 1982. By one of the central figures in Harvard's *Project Zero*, focuses on the artistic development of young children. Includes discussion of the noted child prodigy Nadia, who also suffered from autism, and, as part of a general discussion of her case, takes a critical view of positions that have explained her case on the basis of a right-brain left-brain split of functions. Discussion of children's art is preceded by a lengthy presentation of several points of view on the correctness of a developmental model, among them, Jean Piaget, Noam Chomsky, Claude Lévi-Strauss, and Ernst Cassirer.

Gibson, James J. *The Perception of the Visual World*. Boston: Houghton Mifflin, 1950. Gibson's first major work and the foundation for much of the second chapter of this volume. Though he would modify and expand his position in his later work (this work concentrates on the retinal image), this book lays the groundwork for Gibson's radical view that the environment provides sensory data that is in itself already ordered.

Gibson, James J. *The Senses Considered as Perceptual Systems*. Boston: Houghton Mifflin, 1966. Provides significant modification and breadth to his earlier work, *The Perception of the Visual World*.

Here he gives greater emphasis to the role of both kinesthetic interaction with the environment and the interaction of the senses with each other.

Gibson, James J. *The Ecological Approach to Visual Perception*. Boston: Houghton Mifflin, 1979. Gibson's concluding work, in which he returns to his original focus on visual perception. Study of the role of movement as a constant condition of the observer is used to posit the ambient optical array as a sufficient condition for vision.

Gombrich, E. H. *Art and Illusion*. Princeton: Princeton University Press, 1960. Gombrich's powerful study that considers pictorial representation from the multiple perspectives current in modern psychology. Gombrich draws significantly from Gestalt psychology and transactional empiricism, as well as from the formative work of J. J. Gibson.

Gombrich, E. H. *The Image and the Eye*. Ithaca: Cornell University Press, 1982. Gombrich continues the direction of his earlier work, *Art and Illusion*, but in this volume builds more significantly on the mature work of J. J. Gibson.

Gombrich, E. H. "Meditations on a Hobby Horse," in *Aspects of Form*. Edited by L. L. Whyte. Bloomington: Indiana University Press, 1966, pp. 209–228. Gombrich's oft-cited parable on the mechanisms of representation. This work is key to the formulation of drawing as an act of making that is presented in the first chapter of this volume.

Gregory, R. L. *Eye and Brain*. 3rd ed. New York: McGraw Hill, 1978. Readable volume introducing the broad issues of visual perception. Includes discussion of the physiology of seeing and explanations from various points of view of noted visual illusions and linear perspective.

Ittleson, W. *The Ames Demonstrations in Perception*. Princeton: Princeton University Press, 1952. Documents the noted demonstrations conducted by Adelbert Ames Jr. that have provided significant support for the transactional position.

Koffka, Kurt. *Principles of Gestalt Psychology*. New York: Harcourt Brace, 1935.

Köhler, Wolfgang. *Gestalt Psychology*. New York: H. Liveright, 1929.

Libby, William Charles. *Color and the Structural Sense*. Englewood Cliffs: Prentice-Hall, 1974.

Lobell, John. *Between Silence and Light: Spirit in the Architecture of Louis I. Kahn*. Boulder: Shambhala Publications, 1979.

Lorenz, Konrad. "The Role of Gestalt Perception in Animal and Human Behavior," in *Aspects of Form*. Edited by L. L. Whyte. Bloomington: Indiana University Press, 1966, pp. 157–178. Excellent account of the mechanism of perception as understood from the perspective of Gestalt psychology.

Mayo, Maxwell. *Line and Light*. Pittsburgh: Department of Architecture, Carnegie Mellon University, 1971.

McKim, Robert H. *Experiences in Visual Thinking*. Monterey: Brooks/Cole, 1972. Addresses representation and its relationship to creativity and the design process.

Mendelowitz, Daniel Marcus. *Mendelowitz's Guide to Drawing*. New York: Holt, Reinhart and Winston, 1976. An outstanding and comprehensive text on fine arts drawing.

Nicholaides, Kimon. *The Natural Way to Draw*. Boston: Houghton Mifflin, 1941. Influential book on freehand drawing by a former teacher from Art Students League in New York. Book is foundation for Chapter 1 in this book.

Pirenne, M. H. *Optics, Painting and Photography*. Cambridge: Cambridge University Press, 1970. Optics of both the generation and viewing of perspective drawings. Limitations of perspective as a representation of the visual field are addressed. Includes a description of projective procedures used in executing the ceiling fresco at S. Ignazio by the Pozzo family.

Panofsky, Erwin. "Die Perspektive als Symbolische Form," in *Vorträge der Bibliothek, Warburg, 1924–25* Berlin-Leipzig: 1925, pp. 258–330. Influential paper that presents a critique of perspective on optical and artistic grounds. As for the latter, it considers its limitations both from the well-known position of Plato (i.e., perspective distorts reality) and from his own position: perspective objectifies subjective reality. Panofsky also identifies a paradox of perspective particularly as it develops in Northern Europe, while, on the one hand, it closes pictures from a former religious role as a vehicle of religious symbolic order, it also opens a new role, within the Baroque, as a vehicle of religious vision.

Plato, "The Republic," in the *Dialogues of Plato*, translated into English by B. Jowett. New York: Random House, 1937, pp. 852–879. Plato's influential statements on the limitations of pictorial art.

Segall, Marshall H., Donald T. Campbell, and Melville J. Herskovits. *The Influence of Culture on Visual Perception*. New York: Bobbs Merrill, 1966. Looks at visual perception (and within that some well-known visual illusions) from the stance of cultural relativism.

The Travel Sketches of Louis I. Kahn. Philadelphia: Pennsylvania Academy of Fine Arts, 1978. Presents the travel sketches of Louis I. Kahn from his three trips to the Mediterranean.

Warren, Richard M. and Roslyn P. *Helmholtz on Perception.* New York: John Wiley & Sons, 1968. Presents a brief history of the key nineteenth-century empiricist and forerunner of present-day transactional empiricism, Hermann L. F. Helmholtz. Includes original treatises of Helmholtz on questions of visual perception, together with commentary by the authors on each.

White, John. *The Birth and Rebirth of Pictorial Space.* Boston: Boston Book and Art Shop, 1967. Addresses pictorial space at the critical juncture before and after Brunelleschi's perspective demonstration. Includes discussion of the work of Cimabue, Giotto, Masaccio, Donatello, Ghiberti, Paolo Uccello, and the Sienese masters. It concludes with a brief look back at the pictorial space of imperial Rome, in particular the frescoes of Pompeii.

Winner, Ellen. *Invented Worlds.* Cambridge: Harvard University Press, 1982. Along with Howard Gardner, Ellen Winner is one of the central figures in Harvard's *Project Zero.* The book provides a good overview of psychological issues as they relate to the arts, and is particularly strong in its explanations of children's art.

Wright, L. *Perspective in Perspective.* London: Routledge & Kegan Paul, 1983. In-depth account of the history and techniques of perspective from the Greeks and Romans to the present day. Includes detailed accounts of Alberti's method of generating perspectives with distance points; Piero della Francesca and Paolo Uccello's generation of perspectives from plans; and the Pozzo family's technique for projecting the ceiling fresco at S. Ignazio in Rome.

Glossary

Accommodation. Depth cue conditioned on the eye's changing focal length in viewing objects at various distances.

Atmospheric perspective. Depth cue conditioned on the effect of air on the color and visual acuity of objects at various distances from the observer. Also called aerial perspective.

Axonometric projection. System of projection, including isometry and dimetry. Objects are positioned in an attitude tilted to the picture plane and projected to the picture plane with orthogonal (lines at 90°) sight lines. Axonometric views are drawn to scale, represent all three faces of a rectangular object (front, top, and side), and show parallel lines as parallel.

Bird's eye view. Steeply inclined downward looking perspective view. Bird's-eye views yield a strong sense of the plan of an object or scene.

Center of vision. In perspective drawing, the point at which the viewer is looking on the picture plane.

Chiaroscuro. From the Italian *chiarro*, meaning light, and *oscuro*, meaning dark, a technique of drawing that represents a full range of value from light to dark, typically on a gray background.

Cone of vision. In perspective drawing, a conical field of vision radiating out from the viewer's eyes. Equivalent to the term *breadth of field* as it would be understood by a photographer. Typical cones of vision used in perspective range from 30° to 60° and rarely exceed 90°.

Contour. Lines on the surface of objects generated by profiles, interior edges, and surface textures.

Convergence. 1. Depth cue conditioned on the angle at which the two eyes must converge in viewing an object in close proximity to the viewer. 2. In perspective drawing, the phenomenon of parallel lines appearing to come together at common vanishing points.

Depth cues. Conditions in the visual field that yield a perception of depth. Depth cues are generally divided into two groups: primary cues, which are conditioned on the existence of two eyes, and secondary cues, which are independent of the existence of two eyes.

Dimetric projection. A type of axonometric projection in which two of an object's spatial axes describe equal angles relative to the picture plane.

Disparity vision. Depth cue conditioned on the disparity between the views from the two eyes in viewing objects that are in close proximity to the viewer.

Ecological psychology. An understanding of perception that emphasizes the contribution of the order implicit in the environment. The principal advocate of this position is James J. Gibson.

Elevation. A horizontal directed orthographic view of a vertical face of an object or space.

Empathy. Sharing the same emotions or sensations as another person. In this text, empathy is understood to be transferable to inanimate things.

Foreshortening. The apparent reduction in size of elements on longitudinal surfaces (surfaces that are turned relative to the viewer) with greater distance from the observer.

Gestalt psychology. An understanding of perception that emphasizes the role of predisposing laws in the process of perception.

Ground line. In perspective drawing, a line on the picture plane where the ground plane or assumed ground plane meets the picture plane.

Horizon line. In perspective projection, a line on the picture plane that is level to the ground, passes through the center of vision, and represents the height of the viewer's eyes.

Isometric projection. From the Greek *iso*, meaning same, and *metron*, meaning measure. A type of axonometric projection in which all three of an object's spatial axes describe equal angles relative to the picture plane.

Magic method. A method for constructing one-point perspectives using elevations or sectional views.

Motion parallax. Depth cue conditioned on differences between apparent optical motions of objects at various distances from an observer who is moving.

One-point perspective. The characteristic perspective view resulting from viewing in a direction that is parallel to the major spatial axis of an object or space.

Orthographic projection. System of projection including plans, elevations, and section. Objects are positioned in an attitude parallel to the picture plane and projected to the picture plane with orthogonal (lines at 90°) sight lines. Orthographic views are drawn to scale, show parallel lines as parallel, represent frontal surfaces without distortion of shape or proportion, and represent only one face of a rectangular object (front, top, or side).

Overlap. Depth cue conditioned on near objects overlapping distant objects.

Oblique projection. System of projection that includes plan oblique and elevation oblique views. Objects are positioned in an attitude parallel to the picture plane and projected to the picture plane with *oblique* (lines at angles other than 90") sight lines. Oblique views are drawn to scale, show parallel lines as parallel, represent frontal surfaces without distortion of shape or proportion, and represent all three faces of a rectangular object (front, top, and side). *See also* Paraline views.

Paraline views. Not a system of projection itself but rather a category of projective systems. Includes those systems such as axonometric and oblique projection that show all three faces of objects and at the same time maintain parallel lines as parallel.

Perspective, linear. 1. Depth cue conditioned on the apparent convergence of parallel lines with greater distance from the observer. 2. Drawing system built on the convergent projection of parallel lines to common vanishing points and on the convergent projection of sight lines to a single station point, the position of the viewer.

Pictorial depth cues. Those depth cues that are independent of the existence of two eyes and can be represented on a two-dimensional plane.

Picture plane. A plane, analogous to a window, through which drawing are projected.

Plan. A vertically directed orthographic view of a top or bottom face of an object or space.

Section. A horizontally directed orthographic view into the inside of an object or space.

Shade and shadow. Depth cue predicated on the information provided by shade and shadow.

Sight line. A line used to project points on an object to equivalent positions on a picture plane. Sight lines can vary in their attitude to the picture plane; in orthographic and axonometric projection, they are always orthogonals (at 90°); in oblique projection, they are oblique (at angles other than 90°); in perspective projection, they converge at a single point, the position of the viewer.

Size perspective. Depth cue conditioned on the apparent reduction in size of objects with greater distance from the observer.

Spatial armature. A geometric framework of coordinates on which a drawing can be constructed.

Station point. In perspective projection, the point representing the position of the viewer to which convergent sight lines are drawn.

Surface texture. Term used by James J. Gibson to mean any condition of surface that reflects light that varies from light to dark across its surface.

Textural gradient. Term used by James J. Gibson to mean the condition at the point of impact of light on the retina that corresponds in an ordinal manner (point for point) to the texture from which light has been reflected.

Transactional psychology or transactional empiricism. An understanding of perception that emphasizes the contributions of learning and interaction with the environment to the process of perceiving. Principal advocates of this position are John Dewey and Adelbert Ames.

Two-point perspective. The characteristic perspective view resulting from viewing in a direction that is diagonal to both major spatial axes of an object or space.

Upward position in visual field. Depth cue predicated on the tendency of objects to be seen against the background of a continuous ground or floor surface. Objects that are farther tend to be located higher in the visual field and those that are nearer tend to be located lower in the visual field.

Vertical measuring line. In perspective drawing, a line on the picture plane used to generate vertical information at scale.

Vanishing point. In perspective projection, a point on the picture plane at which a set of parallel lines appears to converge.

Visual field. The sensation of vision projected on the retina; that is, sensation as against perception.

Index